Graham Dalby spent his early years in Africa and Singapore and was educated at Dover College. After a short spell of teaching, he was commissioned as inspector into the Royal Hong Kong Police. Returning to England he spent four years studying music at Trinity College of Music. As a singer, composer and conductor he has toured the world and performed at historic events including the Hong Kong Handover and for the British Royal Family, and those of Monaco and Jordon. He is the founder of the London Swing Orchestra with whom he has toured globally, recorded profusely and broadcast widely from Buckingham Palace to Beijing.

Graham Dalby

Can't Hear Yourself Think

Autobiography of a Serial Name-Dropper

AUSTIN MACAULEY PUBLISHERS™

LONDON • CAMBRIDGE • NEW YORK • SHARJAH

A CIP catalogue record for this title is available from the British Library.

ISBN 9781398460171 (Paperback)
ISBN 9781398460188 (Hardback)
ISBN 9781398460195 (ePub e-book)

www.austinmacauley.com

First Published 2022
Austin Macauley Publishers Ltd®
1 Canada Square
Canary Wharf
London
E14 5AA

Chapter 1
A Close Encounter

The title of this book is taken from an episode which took place in the Waterloo Chamber at Windsor Castle on June 21st 2000, a day which every anti-monarchist and anarchistic terrorist in the world would come to rue as the greatest missed opportunity since Guido Fawkes realised he'd come out without any matches.

I had been invited to play music for dancing with my Swing Orchestra at a party hosted by Her Majesty to honour the 100th birthday of the other majesty, Elizabeth, the Queen Mother, who like Queen Victoria had outlived her husband by half a century. There were other birthdays to celebrate too as Princess Margaret had reached a party-going 70, the Princess Royal a sporty half-century and the Duke of York had notched up a golf-swinging 40. It was then, an occasion when practically every member of every Royal Family around the world was invited, present and correct. There were two other bands also performing. One, the nonagenarian New Yorker called Lester Lanin, who had played at the Queen's 21st birthday party, and a Society London pop-covers band who were served by a very enthusiastic sound crew who also looked after our amplification. We played first and I was very gratified to see that people were dancing, in particular the Queen and Prince Phillip, each with other guests. The Duke seemed pleased to be amusing an attractive brunette with whom he was dancing. After our allocated slot was almost up, I allowed the boys to blow up a bit louder as we came to the big closing numbers of the set. There was enthusiastic applause from the floor and up strode the board-backed Duke straight to the stage. I stood and beamed awaiting the compliments that must surely be showered upon the director of this august body of musicians. "Can't hear yourself think in here!" was the inevitable put-down. We slunk off the stage in ignominious retreat from what we had perceived to be a great success, routed for having played too loudly so as to interrupt the witty Royal Repartee that was holding his dance partner in sway. No MBE for me then?

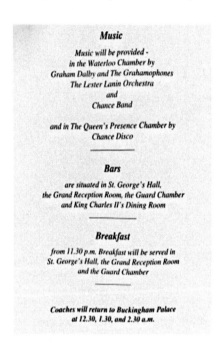

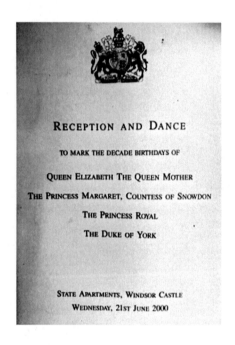

I remained to listen to the New York band of aged jazz veterans and consoled myself by downing a few glasses of State Apartments fizz. I was fascinated to hear this band of which I had heard so many socialite party-planning ladies rave. This band, apparently, could play through the night without stopping; no gaps between numbers and no breaks for the orchestra. It was a musician's idea of utter purgatory. Lady Elizabeth Anson, the Queen's cousin and owner of the society agency, Party Planners, had brought over the band at the last minute as a surprise present to the Queen. I rather guessed that she had been more than a little irked when the Master of the Household, being a military man and not having too much knowledge of bands or parties, decided to refer back to the splendid work that Colonel Blair Stuart-Wilson did in organising 'The Four Royal Birthdays' at Buckingham Palace in 1990 when the Queen Mother turned 90. He himself told me that he had consulted the foremost royal with a real appreciation of music, Princess Margaret, and she had suggested my orchestra following a party for the Devonshire's at Chatsworth. So that's how I found myself getting re-booked as it were. The American band had had their difficulties in getting flights over at such short notice and could not possibly get work visas in time so they would not be bringing their instruments lest questions were asked at customs. They were, in effect, planning to perform illegally for the Royal Family. I was astonished, a few days before the ball, to field a phone call in my south-of-the-river home from Lady Elizabeth herself asking whether they might be able to borrow our instruments! I was shocked, as anyone who knows anything of professional musicians would understand how personal their instruments are to them and the idea of lending them to complete strangers was inconceivable, almost like sharing your toothbrush with a stranger. I suggested the best option was to hire them in England but stressed that the quality would be very basic. And that is just what they did.

I watched intently as the small band took its place and noticed that they had no music stands. Were they going to play the whole set for memory? Oh yes, and not only that, they played continuous hooked-on Cole Porter type songs with no beginning and no end, all busking the tune mostly at the same tempo irrespective of the song. The fact that they were playing on third-rate instruments didn't help either. So, we had *Night and Day*, *Anything Goes*, *I've got you under my skin* all segued into each other and held together by the perpetual boom-cha of the brushes on the snare drum. This wasn't just dull; it was like listening to a speech by a politician after he had just perfected the art of rotary breathing. The nonagenarian band leader, Lester Lanin, had previously asked me what the Queen Mother's favourite song was during the afternoon and I replied that I knew she liked *A Nightingale Sang in Berkeley Square* but added that it was in our set-list prior to him coming on. Notwithstanding, this song popped up, in the same tempo as all the other songs they played, no less than five times.

Whilst I was standing there, conspicuous in my trademark white dinner jacket, champagne glass in hand, watching as Lady Elizabeth cajoled people onto the dance floor, a terrible thing happened as frightening as anything I can recall. Bearing down towards the corner, where I was propping up a pillar, was a diminutive figure with a bearing and charisma so perfect that her aura filled the room. The Queen of England, 'Regina Elizabetha' no less, was heading straight towards me! I am actually the very worst dancer on the planet and the wide genial smile on her face, so often photographed in serious pose, and her sparkling eyes had all the attributes of one who wished to dance with everybody in the room. I was caught like the oft-quoted bunny in the headlights, unable to move, riveted to the spot. Her eyes met momentarily with mine and then as if some divine right of kings (or queens) sixth sense warned her of my abject fear of dancing, she turned at the last moment like a glancing arrow and invited the poor stiff on my right to join her for the next dance. He also proved a turkey but there, I thought, for the grace of God…I beat a hasty retreat away from the dance floor and into another chamber.

It was here that I experienced first-hand how fabulously snobbish and un-egalitarian American socialites can be. A clever and beautiful guest of the Duke of York (who I believe to have been the glamorous brain specialist Dr Melanie Walker) greeted me with the single syllable greeting so favoured by our American cousins:

"Hi…!"

"How d' you do?" I replied. I never found out as she quickly moved onto the question that seemed to be uppermost in her mind.

"So, who do you know here?"

That was an easy one for me as most of the guests were quite recognisable figures.

"Ah!" I said. "Well, that tall chap looking uncomfortable in uniform and medals is the Crown Prince of Norway and that good-looking fellow over there is Anthony Andrews, the actor, talking to Peregrine Armstrong-Jones and I think that is Princess Xenia of Hohenlohe-Langen talking to Prince Gustav zu Sayn-Wittgenstein-Berleberg and Princess Badiya El Hassan of Jordon and…oh! Good evening your Grace!"

An elderly gentleman shook my hand.

"Have you seen my wife?"

"Sorry?"

"Forgive me; I'm having a senior moment. Aren't you that band-leader chappie who played for us at Chatsworth and we saw you playing later that year at Buckingham Palace?"

"That's right, it's Dalby, Graham Dalby."

"Oh, yes I do recall, splendid, splendid, well if you see her please tell her I've found her handbag!" And he tottered off in search of the Duchess of Devonshire.

I turned to the American socialite and was about to apologise for the lack of an introduction as we ourselves had not yet disclosed our own names.

"That was the Duke of Dev…" I broke off startled by the look of abject horror on her face. "Did he say you're a musician? A…bandleader!" She blanched.

"Oh yes," I beamed.

"Oh my Gaaahd!" With the look of one who has just discovered a slug in her salad, she turned on her heel and walked off in the direction of some other guests that included the jazz musicians Johnny Dankworth and Dame Cleo Laine.

Twenty years later in 2020, I was called by a journalist and asked about this party, in particular, whether Melanie Walker, Ghislaine Maxwell and Jeffrey Epstein attended this auspicious ball. At the time I had no idea who they were and cared less. The short answer, however, was yes, they were and this is now the subject of intense media investigation.

Chapter 2
Out of Africa – 1958
Long Odds on Survival

Mary with Baby Graham – Nigeria 1958

I was born at the Royal Engineers Hospital in Chatham, the third of four children. My father, as a serving army officer, had been decorated in Korea, Palestine and Malta, working in the insanely hazardous world of bomb disposal. Not content with UXB work in Malta, he specialised in underwater bomb disposal and helped clear the Suez Canal of mines. He had lived something of a charmed life, having survived 'The Battle of the Imjin River' and being shot at by Zionist terrorists whilst serving with the Arab Legion in Palestine. Shortly after I was born, he left these life-threatening adventures for pastures new as a colonial ex-pat in Nigeria. He took the family with him and started a new life working for a timber company.

It was here, stationed about two hundred miles from the nearest European that I began the first year of my life. There exists a faded colour photo of me, as a tiny blond baby, nestling contentedly on the shoulder of the nanny named Mary in front of the veranda that formed the front of our ranch-like house in the Nigerian Bush.

My father was now in the timber business and worked alongside the local workforce through the efficient control of the foreman, the local head honcho, who was as fiercely loyal as he was fierce to behold. His face was marked with the three scars that are a feature of the Yoruba culture but apparently, he adored me and it was very much vice-versa.

Now, it came to pass that my father and the foreman had to go away for a few days to inspect the lumber estate that covered a vast area. The security of the house and grounds were left in the dubiously incapable hands of a towering young buck of the Igbo people with very fixed ideas as to the social standing of women. Within minutes of the dust dying away, as the company's Land Rover's suspension was being put to the severest test, our new young deputy foreman settled down to enjoy his recent promotion in the hammock on our private lawn, such as it was. An hour passed, and then another, as he dozed away in the warm African afternoon in blissful, somnolent indolence. This, he must have thought, was the life. His tranquillity was suddenly disturbed by what he perceived as the loud buzzing of an angry bee and he sleepily waved his hand in a dismissive gesture, annoyed at having his repose so rudely disrupted. His eyelids opened heavily to see that, silhouetted against the hot sun, was the diminutive figure of the boss's wife, my mother or Mutti as she was to become universally known and by which name I shall refer to her henceforth throughout this book.

"Ahhm de Bossman hee now. You jus wohman. You go keeetchen now not tell me what to do! You go tell Mary, she help you."

Now, anyone who has the smallest inkling of the classic character trait of the women that held together both India and vast swathes of Africa and the Far East would have winced at this rebuff in the knowledge that this lad was about to be on the receiving end of the full wrath of an outraged Colonial Memsahib. With Mutti, it was the work of a moment to send the utterly astonished, lanky figure spinning out of the hammock and plummeting downwards through the three-foot drop onto the hard-baked turf below. Having made her point quite concisely, Mutti turned to return to the kitchen where Mary was holding me and looking wide-eyed, having seen what Mutti had not. The young buck, his pride and his

11

buttocks, having suffered something of an equal bruising, was sufficiently recovered and having loped off to grab a panga (machete), was now heading at full tilt towards the kitchen, eyes blazing with murderous intent. Slamming through the fly-door with raised panga, the kitchen then played host to a trio of simultaneously raised voices. Our volatile young lad, all six foot two of him, was giving vent to his rage by bellowing in his native dialect concerning his immediate plans for Mutti and probably me as well. Mary was screaming and trying to act as interpreter along the lines of:

"Oh Madam! He say he kill you! He kill you, Madam!"

Mutti stood her ground like a rugby full-back and remained cool under fire, pointing to the door with the repost.

"Get out of my kitchen!"

Given that there was a baby and my young sister Hilary, aged five, to defend and no one there to help her, this was indeed a tense moment. There are several things Mutti shares with the Queen: similar age, height (5'2") and most fortunately for me, an imperious look that could open an oyster at 40 paces. Most of the ranting had been in the direction of Mary but he now turned to look at Mutti and that was when he caught her eye with that look. It would have given a charging wildebeest pause for thought and our Igbo friend lost heart and slunk off with a sulky parting shot. "When bossman get back, I tell him, he beat you good!"

In this, our hot-headed young buck had displayed a woeful lack of comprehension of the calibre of the British Memsahib and the healthy respect accorded to them by their menfolk in the colonies. On the return of my father and the fierce-looking foreman, the lad was dismissed and apparently handed a bit of hiding by the foreman; a no-nonsense head of the community who went on to become a colonel in the Nigerian army after Independence. There was no love lost between the Yoruba and the Igbo peoples of Nigeria. The buck retired into private life. This may well have been a close call for my future, but a much closer call was to follow just a very short time later...

What was not known or understood at this time was that, having survived the panga attack, however much hot air it turned out to be, a really genuinely life-threatening situation was fast developing from which the chances of survival were practically non-existent. I was developing respiratory problems, and far more worrying, I had begun to change colour. No longer a pretty pink but as a pale powder-blue baby, I became the subject of grave concern.

Atrial Septal Defect (ASD) was sometimes known as a 'hole in the heart' and was often but not always, a fatal condition. If the small hole in the heart, which enables the blood of the unborn baby to pass from the left atrium of the heart to the right, whilst by-passing the lungs and allowing the baby to receive oxygen from the placenta, fails to close upon birth, a blood overload in the right atrium can cause an enlargement on the right side and eventually, heart failure. This is because the left atrium is oxygen-heavy and has the task of pumping blood to the entire body whereas the right side only needs enough to supply blood to the now activated lungs. If the shunt is from left to right then you get an overload and heart failure but, if the shunt is from right to left, the oxygen-poor blood from the right atrium will be pumped around the body causing low blood oxygen and cyanosis will occur. Cyanosis is a blue discolouring of the skin caused by deoxygenation of the blood and it was probably this that gave me the cyan hue.

My father took this rapidly declining baby bundle and headed off in the Land Rover to the nearest hospital, a short drive of some two hundred miles over mostly dirt tracks or very poor roads to the town of Ibadan. Now, Ibadan had some pros and cons going for it. Firstly, it had a hospital and an hotel. Secondly, and very importantly, it had an airport. But, thirdly, it had an outbreak of plague so that the children's ward was full of seriously sick children. A distraught and frazzled Army doctor was working desperately through the night with Nigerian doctors and nurses when he was suddenly presented with a white baby sporting a rather fetching hint of powder blue. My condition was way beyond his knowledge or skills and he shook his head ruefully as I was placed in the ward. My father was left to check in to one of the two hotels. Had he chosen the other hotel things would have gone very differently.

His son, strangely sick and in a plague-infested hospital, in what was then a third-world hospital, I think my father could be forgiven for heading straight to the hotel bar (not that he ever needed an excuse) for a late-night drink. A weary barman was waiting patiently for his one customer to go so that he might close up. The solo European was delighted to get some company and as the somnambulist barman poured out the whisky, my father poured out his heart on the subject of his gravely ill baby boy. Now, the fact that this one total stranger, in the middle of nowhere, turned out to be a Swiss physician who had made a study of the pioneering 'Catheter Procedure' rather than using highly risky open-heart surgery does, I must confess, beggar belief. While my father was famous for telling stories taller than those of Baron Munchausen, I am alive and I do have a small scar where the tiny umbrella was inserted into a vein in the groin and fed through to the septum to close the hole. I also have an indentation in the ribcage at the sola-plexus consistent with the heart losing pressure, so I know much of this must be true.

Within the time it takes to down a large whisky, they were both in a taxi, much to the relief of the barman, and shortly after, my father was identifying his son as the only one who was not only pink but also blue. Within minutes, I was out of the ward and was being ferried to the hotel where the Swiss physician was busy sending urgent telegrams to his colleagues in London. A short flight from Ibadan and a connecting flight from Lagos to London, with an ambulance on the tarmac, ensured that less than a day had elapsed and I was in the operating theatre of the greatest children's hospital in the world, Great Ormond Street. Apart from being a logistics expert, my saviour also knew one of the only men in England capable of such an operation and had patched through a call from Ibadan to his home in London in the middle of the night. He and his team of specialists were standing by as my ambulance pulled into Tavistock Square. I was later to learn that the surgeon was none other than the Queen's paediatrician, a Dr Philip Evans. The young ticker held out, the operation was a success and six months later, I was declared fit to carry on. I think that I already had had my fair share of good fortune from that early age but…I was going to need plenty more.

Chapter 3
Singapore 1965 – More Life-Threatening Adventures

Curry Lunch at The Gap in Singapore with baby Python (Little girl behind prodding sleeping Cobra!)

Five quiet years slipped by in what, from the photographs, seemed to be an idyllic world of late 50s England where Mutti sported large 50s style sunglasses and polka-dot dresses and my father had a pale blue convertible Hillman Minx and it was, of course, always summer. The fifty-fifty chance the doctors had given me had gone in my favour and by the age of six, I had no recollection of what had gone before. My father had made little headway in Civvy Street after leaving Africa on my account and decided that his best bet was to return to the Services. Unable to rejoin the Army due to his age, the RAF had no such qualms and was keen to recruit an experienced engineer to head-up a squadron for airfield construction. And so it was that I found myself in the windy, cabbage-smelling fenlands of RAF Water beach. It was here, one Saturday afternoon, that my father returned home, late for lunch, having the demeanour of the cat that had got the cream or had enjoyed a good session in the Officers Mess. Mutti, having clearly missed the amusing part of his keeping us waiting for lunch, waved an official letter from an exasperated bank manager and was astonished to see him read the letter with mock concern before tearing the missive in two and tossing the fragments into the air.

"To hell with the bank manager!" He laughed. "We've been posted"– he paused for dramatic effect – "four years…in Singapore!"

I joined in the whooping and cheering with gusto, not having the smallest idea of what any of this meant but I just enjoyed adding to the jubilant noises. The newest addition to the family, my brother John, aged two, threw his plastic mug across the floor in a show of unity, we knew what he meant.

Soon the garden began to fill with stout tea-chests filled with straw and Mutti, a veteran of some two dozen moves, began to pack down the OMQ (Officer's Married Quarter). I lost count of the number of times I was carted off to the MO to have both arms stuck like a pin-cushion with every inoculation known to science. Singapore might be an oriental paradise but it was once a swamp drained by the great Sir Stamford Raffles. Her Majesty's colonial servants were given every possible medical protection ranging from Malaria, Cholera, Tuberculosis, Diphtheria, Yellow Fever, Scarlet Fever, Denghi Fever, and, I think, everything from Beriberi to Tennis Elbow and Housemaid's knee. To place the time more accurately, my eldest sister, Sheran, had almost worn out her Beatles EP's with deeply evocative titles such as *I wanna hold your hand* or the even more disturbingly profound *She loves you, Yeah*. But, as if these lyrical gems were not enough for 60s kiddies, onto our black and white screens every Saturday afternoon came the terrifying BBC electronic workshop masterpiece that was the spine-tingling theme from the very first episodes of Dr Who. I raged in disbelief as I realised that I would miss finding out what happened to the doctor and his friends captured and held in the City of the Daleks. They had just blinded and incapacitated a Dalek and just as something nasty began to emerge from within the robotic shell, up came the credits with the wailing unearthly music. I never saw the following episode but I later saw the colour film re-make with Peter Cushing and Roy Castle (the trumpet player). Decades later in another era with the actor Roy Castle taken tragically early to cancer, his son Ben Castle, a fine saxophonist, came and played in a function band I was running and I recounted the story. However, back to 1964…

We left England on December 1ˢᵗ on a freezing cold evening for the first leg of our journey on an Eagle Airways Britannia, one of the last great turboprop aircraft, en-route for Rome. By the time the aircraft had roared off into the Italian night sky over the Aegean and Eastwards to India, I was deep in the arms of Morpheus and curled up as only a child can in the confines of an aeroplane. I awoke to bright sunlight, orange juice and a smiling stewardess holding a small cake with an unlit candle. It was my seventh birthday! The birthday seemed to last forever, through Istanbul, Bombay and finally, finally, we began our descent onto the island of Singapore. Mutti offered her condolences to a frazzled mother whose young child had screamed most of the way and who, incredibly, had to remain on board for the long onward haul to Perth. The first effect of disembarkation into the tropics is one of disbelief, as the heat hits you, and then a despairing realisation that you are wearing the wrong clothes.

After being whisked through immigration, we were driven to a splendidly classical colonial hotel. It wasn't The Raffles for sure but having just escaped the cold, wet winter fenlands of Cambridge, the immensely rich and exotic fauna of the gardens framing a beautiful white hotel with balconies, verandas and bamboo furniture, seemed everything I had ever dreamt of. Under the incessant wogga-wogga of the overhead fans, diligent, white-gloved waiters, seemingly impervious to the heat, brought trays of tea or more often, gin and tonics to ex-patriot ladies already acclimatised to the intense tropical swelter and humidity.

For my father, there was no chance to rest and he was at once introduced to his C.O. who escorted him away to see his new office. Whilst Mutti and my siblings flaked out in their room, I determined to waste no time in exploring. I soon chummed up with a Chinese boy my own age, whose father was the hotel manager, and he showed me, a very willing student, how to make lethal weapons out of bamboo. Before long I was like a character out of Lord of the Flies. This, I thought to myself, was going to be great!

Singapore in those last halcyon days of Empire still retained much of the old-world charm as experienced by Noël Coward, Evelyn Waugh or Douglas Fairbanks Jnr. when they visited. Coward never mentions Singapore in his song *Mad Dogs and Englishmen* (probably because Hong Kong was easier to rhyme) but The Raffles Hotel has a suite named in his honour along with their own cocktail, the Singapore Sling, which Coward enjoyed immensely. India may have gone but it was as if the entire British Raj decamped to Singapore to carry on as before. This was a multicultural haven of Chinese (Hok-Yuen and Cantonese speakers), Malays, Indians, South Africans and a whole myriad of flotsam and jetsam washed up and marooned by the ebbing tide of the British Empire. The terrible Fall of Singapore to the Japanese in 1942 was an indelible stain on British pride and you couldn't help feeling that, to the local Chinese population, the memory of that shameful capitulation was still green, as were the memories of the terrible atrocities perpetrated on them by the invading forces. At that time (December '64), Winston Churchill had just over a month left to live and I have heard it said, that his incredulity of learning, whilst sat in President Roosevelt's office in the White House, that 100,000 British and Empire soldiers had lain down their arms to 30,000 Japanese troops on bicycles, would go with him to his dying day. It came on January 24th 1965 and I witnessed, without quite understanding what all the huge fuss was about, the funeral of the great man at Westminster Abbey. It was broadcast all day on every channel in every conceivable language and dialect from all four corners of the Empire. I felt oddly proud to be a part of that but was soon bored by the constant replays of the cortège, so I went out to play in the rain. All I can recall is rescuing my little brother who I thought was performing some exotic rain-dance but it transpired that he had disturbed an anthill and enraged millions of its occupants (rather like the British in India perhaps?).

I saw a little something of myself, so many years later, when I went to the cinema to watch Spielberg's 'Empire of the Sun', in the self-assured, hyper-active boy on his bicycle in Shanghai. When he returns to the empty house after the Japanese had taken Shanghai, his Amah gives him the huge slap around the face that she had been longing to do for years. I'm sure my Amah would have gladly dispensed the same to me if she had thought she might have got away with it. I would cycle off for hours to Malay and Chinese Kampongs and marvel at the squalor in which these poor, desperate people lived. The villages shared a double tap for washing whilst pigs and dogs wandered around sharing the mud with little children. The air was constantly heavy with the smell of charcoal fires and boiling clothes or rice. The smells of these places were so varied and have never left me. If I close my eyes, I can still conjure up foul-smelling Durian fruit or unfeasibly sweet rambutans (lychee) and hear the click of the chit-chats (lizards) and the vocalisations of huge basso frogs in the sweltering nights. The night air buzzed with an incessant hum of insect blood predators and a veritable orchestra of crickets. The Malays built their wooden homes on stilts for safety and underneath kept a mongoose as insurance against the fiercely head-tattooed king cobra, an even match in any fight. The smell of the huge, endless chains of blood-red and gold firecrackers and the dreadfully violent late-night Chinese operas…all these became a part of the life of the little boy with a bicycle, a pair of shorts and flip-flops.

One great pleasure was the fun in haggling with the Indian shopkeepers down obscure back-streets. I was sure no respectable person would ever go down there, yet they sold such items as only Europeans would buy; inflatable lilos or boats or beach balls or water pistols. I was very much taken one day by a huge repeating machine-gun water pistol but had only half the money required from the price tag. The Indian tradesman, never one to lose a sale, saw that I had just about half in my grubby palm. He suggested I pay half now and return next week with the balance and with an astonishing lack of business acumen, gave me the toy to take home. I cycled home with this huge plastic gun with a very strong feeling that, if I did not come back, I would jeopardise the entire basis of trust upon which the Empire had been founded. I honestly believed this! I did return with the balance, having had great difficulty in finding the place again in the maze of very similar shops. I took great pride in seeing his wide, black-toothed grin and his turbaned head rocking approvingly from shoulder to shoulder. I realised that I hadn't even haggled but given such trust, I felt I had upheld the honour of my tribe.

A tropical paradise it might have been but…

I'm not quite sure how but I seemed to have developed something of a knack for landing myself in dangerous situations. It was 1965 and my father had been away in Borneo in a place called Kuching where, for some reason, we were waging a war with some communist guerrillas with the help of a very brave friend who my father often referred to as Johnny Gurkha. For reasons best known to the MOD my father arrived directly from his flight to our house, unchanged from his combat gear, and sporting full jungle fatigues, webbing and a service revolver. He had probably brought a few leeches along for the ride. I was so excited to see him but, before the hugs, understandably, he wished to get showered and changed as soon as possible and Mutti fully concurred. Curiosity killed the cat and jolly nearly me. I so wanted to have a peek at that gun. There it was on the bed and just crying out for a little boy to remove it from its webbing holster. Holding the butt of a Smith and Weston .38 service revolver my trigger finger was, mercifully, too small to reach the trigger. I aimed the revolver at the banana tree outside the window. I was impersonating a gun with shooting noises when, to my deep consternation, there was a very real and sudden crack. I felt myself flying across the bedroom and the revolver was snatched from my grasp. There followed one of those Looney-Toon moments, complete with stars and twittering birds, and, for a moment, my hearing was reduced to a high-pitched whistle. As I recovered, I could hear that Mutti had entered, stage left, and a heated altercation was now in progress. As my senses returned it became clear that I had received a hefty clout from my father who had returned from the shower to find me in possession of an, incredibly, still loaded revolver. My father was now on the receiving end of a full matriarchal fusillade similar perhaps to the one that had subdued the panga-wielding buck in Nigeria. As my hearing gradually returned I picked up the gist of the story. It transpired that this was not the first time my father had been careless in bringing his work back home with him.

It was in Malta in the late 50s as a young Royal Engineers Bomb Disposal officer, my father had been decorated for bravery but not before he nearly blew up Mutti and thereby threatened my life before it had even begun – she was expecting me at the time! After a long hot dusty day defusing some of the huge quantity of unexploded ordnance dropped by the Luftwaffe during the siege of Malta, my father was running late for a mess do. Rushing home to shower, he asked Mutti to run an iron over his crumpled khaki trousers. Ever the perfect Army wife, it was with Mutti the work of a moment before a hot iron was restoring the creases to the legwear when it stopped with a metallic clunk against something in the pocket. Removing the offending item, Mutti hung up the perfectly pressed trousers and placed the test-tube shaped object on the bed. My father dressed quickly; his sunburnt face now ashen. It seems that the item was a detonator from a large German bomb he had diffused earlier that day that he had slipped into his pocket and forgotten about.

Returning back now to Singapore, a year or so after the little incident with the revolver, I had by this time, developed all sorts of useful skills. Apart from being a very strong swimmer, I could fry an egg on a panga, pick up a snake without getting bitten, could climb anything like a gecko and was practically immune to mosquitoes.

It happened on a very hot and still afternoon in a place called Pasa-Panjang where we lived by the sea, overlooking Shell Island. Everybody and everything with any sense was having a lie down in the shade, including the gardener, as the heat was intense at that time of day. Everyone, that is, except me. At the base of a leaning 50-foot palm tree, the gardener had left his panga and a converted inner tube with a belt clasp. He was clearly preparing to climb the tree to make safe the huge green coconut husks, the size of basketballs that were in danger of dropping. I gazed up at the immense tree feeling like Jack approaching the beanstalk. It was there like Everest, to be conquered and my natural propensity for danger drew me like a magnet to the panga and the tyre. Attaching the rubber ring around the tree and closing the clasp behind my back, I began the great ascent. Using feet, knees and one hand, the other clutching the panga, I shinned up slowly and painfully. At about 25 feet, I stopped to wipe the sweat from trickling into my eyes. It was at this point that I noticed the fierce sun glinting off a huge silver net emanating from a massive hydrangea bush with purple flowers, six feet from the base of the tree. Because of the angle of the sun, I had not taken in that the terminus of this great silver net was in fact the top of my palm tree. I continued my great ascent until I reached the height where I could hack at the stem of the coconuts. Behind me was a sheer drop of some 40 feet and both my hands were engaged in holding and hacking the husk. It was at this critical moment when I was considering the wisdom of trusting my life to a dodgy piece of old inner-tube when the gargantuan owner of the silver net emerged to see what the hell was going on to disturb his siesta. As an avid Natural Historian, I am sure that at a distance, this was a beautiful and magnificent member of his species. But at 12 inches from my nose, this was a massive arachnid, somewhat larger than a man's spread hand, who ate birds for a living and had a set of truly fearsome mandibles which viewed at close quarters from below, were far worse than any high-tech horror film I have ever seen since. Dropping my panga over my shoulder and throwing myself backwards to put some space between me and those horrible mandibles, I executed perfectly the wrong way to go down a palm tree together with my life-saving inner tube. The abrasions I suffered to my stomach, chest, thighs, ankles and hands were really quite impressive. I peered up to the tree to get a more perspective view of my recent, horrifying acquaintance but he had shuffled back to his siesta.

Many years later, on a warm summer's afternoon, while reading the Hobbit to my young English class at Tormore School in Kent, I was aware of the children's faces contorting at Tolkien's horrific description of Shelob, the giant spider, and it all came flooding back to me. I thought to myself, "Shall I tell them? No, I doubt they'd ever believe me."

Having failed to kill myself in the ballistics and steeple-jack departments, the next possible threat to my safety came from a very different but equally hazardous species of the natural world. Having had a narrow escape from a giant eight-foot sea-snake, spotted by a vigilant lifeguard at The Changi Club several months before, I found myself once more at the mercy of Singapore's fabulously exotic sea life. We had hired a launch for a Sunday to go out to the islands and some friends had joined us. We anchored off a small island in about 40 feet of the clearest crystal warm water and I began agitating for a swim whilst lunch was being prepared. I was told the currents were dangerously strong but nothing is more irritating than a child who wants something badly and I was that child. The grown-ups capitulated. I was told to keep hold of a long rope attached to the boat and never let go whatever. One of my father's friends had just bought a top of the range glass-faced snorkel for a lot of money but he said that I was welcome to borrow it if I took great care to bring it back safely. I slipped over the side of the boat with the mask adjusted to my tiny head and floated just below the surface to observe the unbelievable aquarium in those glistening shallows. The water was so warm and I relaxed my grasp on the rope periodically to feel the strong pull of the current as the rope slipped between my fingers as more and more interesting sights hove into view. Then there came a sight that really grabbed my undivided attention. A huge Polyphemus Horseshoe-Crab directly below, with a vast 36" shell, the size of a coffee table was ambling his way along the sea-bed creating a beautiful pattern in the sand behind him. These strange prehistoric crustaceans, some four hundred and fifty million years old, inhabit the shallow waters. Although it is called a crab, it has no claws and its spider-like body is covered by a horseshoe-shaped shell with a long, spiky tail protruding from behind. So fascinated was I by this alien-looking creature, that I continued floating above it, occasionally loosening my grasp on the rope to keep up with its ponderous progress. It continued on, oblivious of me floating above just as I, in turn, remained in blissful ignorance of a sleek, dark, silent shape that had been observing me for a few minutes at a distance of about 50 yards. I soon came to the end of the long rope attached to the boat and I surfaced to remove the uncomfortable mouthpiece and get my bearings. I was surprised to see I was quite a distance from the boat but I could see that there was some sort of commotion going on deck with a good deal of arm-waving. With the mask now above my forehead, I started to reel myself in and could feel that someone was pulling the rope quite urgently to speed up my progress. I closed in on the vessel quickly until I came within earshot and could make out what was being shouted by several people all at the same time, something about not letting go and hurrying up and something else but what? Shark?? "You are joking!" I was too young to swear but…with a sudden racing pulse, I spun around 360 degrees, treading water and scanning the rippling surface in all directions. I suddenly saw the end of the rope pull past me and I swam sidestroke with an outstretched arm to try and catch it back from the idiot who was pulling it in. I was making little headway against the current when looking back over my shoulder I saw him. There he was, not 50 feet away, and moving slowly with the shiny grey dorsal fin breaking the surface every few seconds. And then it disappeared. The boat was about 50 feet away and I would have no chance in a straight race even with such a head start. Panic is not something you like to admit to but just then and there it seemed the only option.

Throwing off the mask and snorkel I put my head into the water and kicked into the fastest sprint crawl I was capable of. The sound waves transmitted to a shark by kicking and splashing translate as a creature in distress and an easy meal. Notwithstanding, I did not surface until my arm hit against the side of the vessel and two strong hands hauled me out of the water. I turned around the second my feet hit the deck expecting to see a *Jaws*-type Great White crash into the side of the boat in a scene from a film that wouldn't be made for another ten years. The shark had resurfaced and was still a hundred and fifty feet away and was leaving the scene. Apparently, it had been a baby Grey Reef Shark, about five feet long, and who was as fascinated by me as I had been by my horseshoe crab and was startled by my sudden and violent evacuation of the scene. I doubt I would have made much of a meal in any event.

Chapter 4
Alma Mater

Eylesdon Court Prep School – Bearsted, Kent

Sadly, all good things come to an end and, as I was regarded as a bit of a handful, it was decided that the time had come to pack me off to boarding school. Where they found this school, I could never guess, probably recommended by some bloke my father met in the Mess. Anyway, Eylesdon Court Preparatory School for boys turned out to be a beautiful white Georgian house on the green of an obscure and idyllic Kent village, complete with oast houses, called Bearsted. I arrived four days early due to the limited Army flights and spent my first night sleeping alone in a dormitory of 20 empty beds. I found this experience pretty uncomfortable as the only other occupants of this large spooky house, the Head and his wife, occupied a wing over the far side of the building. The upside of this was that when the rest of the school arrived, I didn't feel like a new boy at all and could tell the eight and nine-year-olds, who had not boarded before, to stop blubbing on pain of a pillow-bashing. It was a traditional old boarding school with the Headmaster being a Welsh Latin scholar with thrashings if you didn't learn your declensions and respect if you made the school teams. At weekends, a tough Aussie history master would take the dozen or so boys, whose parents lived overseas on trips to castles all over Southern England on the school bus. It was from him at this time, that I attribute my lifetime fascination with British history. I spent four happy years at this school where I also developed a great love of cricket and rugby. Sadly, despite the floggings, much of my Latin is now forgotten.

Yet again, my comfort zone was compromised. The new Labour government guidelines put massive pressure on my little prep school and soon I was told that the boarding would have to close. I was a year too young to start at my chosen Public School so I was told that I would have to go to their prep school in Folkestone for my Common Entrance year. Moving to a new school at this stage was horrendous.

My little brother, who had always listened intently to my boarding school tales from my wonderful school and who was now looking forward to the experience, joined me. The new prep school I can only describe as absolutely ghastly and the housemaster in charge of the hundred or so boarders turned out to be an Anglo-Catholic who was later ordained into the Roman Catholic clergy. He seemed to take pleasure in making the boys' stay as uncomfortable as possible. He took an immediate dislike to my shell-shocked nine-year-old brother and by contrast, an unhealthy liking to me. I was promoted to school prefect despite the fact I had only been there a matter of weeks and I spent a difficult year trying to keep my brother out of trouble in the face of a persistent campaign by the housemaster to find fault in everything he did. I shan't dwell on this unhappy time but my brother remained behind unprotected while I moved up to public school.

After prep school, the move up was startling insofar as you were suddenly regarded quite differently. It was as if you had suddenly come of age like a Jewish Bah-mitzvah. You could walk out of the gates by yourself, attend coffee bars in town or go shopping and the House was governed by the Head of House and his prefects who kept a watchful eye on bullying.

Dover College then was an all-boys second division public school that boasts a varied assortment of notable alumni including the incomparable choreographer Sir Frederick Ashton and the 21-year-old Captain WP 'Billie' Neville (Head Boy), who was killed at the Somme in 1916, leading his men over the top kicking a football to the German trenches, also notable for very different reasons, Jeffrey Archer (Staff), and Simon Cowell (Leamington House), one year my junior. The

25

school was founded in 1871 and built on the ruined shell of the old Priory of St Martin that was partly destroyed in 1547 when Henry VIII and Thomas Cromwell were busy nationalising the monasteries. The great refectory, the pilgrims rest quarters and some broken cloisters were all that remained of the magnificent flint priory that had played host to Kings, Princes and Archbishops sailing to and from France. King Stephen had died there in 1154. During the 1540s, the great Thomas Tallis, sometimes called the Father of English music, had been organist there.

The first term at public school is always the toughest as most of us had come from being prefects at the top of the pecking order in our previous schools. It came as quite a shock to find ourselves the lowest of the low, a fag. Not what the Americans mean! Fagging was a system whereby the junior boys were required to do valet duties for the sixth form prefects. It was a reward for prefectorial duties but has long since been abolished.

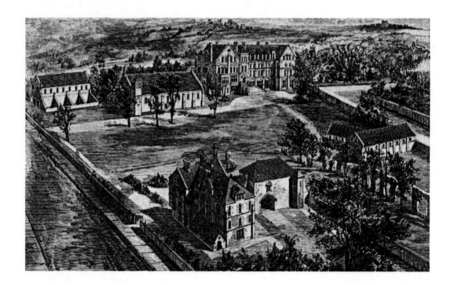

I was in School House and the Head Boy was a tall, very blond, healthy-looking chap called Perkins. A natural leader, he was captain of the 1st XV and had been offered a Sandhurst scholarship. Whenever the Head congratulated the rugby team, he would blush profusely much to the amusement of us rowdy younger lads. Under his guidance, the House was devoid of Flashman-style bullying and we fags did our chores without complaint. The first term was slipping away uneventfully but my major concern was my poor progress in

Mathematics and the devil to pay when my father read my first term exam results. Then, something extraordinary happened that would change my whole life.

Earlier in the term, the Director of Music, a highly flamboyant and eccentric Fellow of the Royal College of Organists, had announced to a very bored music appreciation class that the school orchestra was desperately short of violas. Should anyone wish to take up this instrument the school was offering free tuition for one year. I'd never heard of a viola but thought that an instrument might fill the long Sunday afternoons. I volunteered and thus began the long, agonising process of learning an instrument from scratch. Later, that same term, the Director of Music followed up his advantage. Being 13, my voice had not so much broken as plummeted. After a mercifully short period of my speech, changing pitch from basso profundo to high falsetto four or five times in a sentence, it quickly settled at a reassuringly low baritone pitch and I felt comfortable with this new found masculinity.

I remember one lad, whose voice broke into a deep basso earlier than mine, could now imitate a contented bull. His name, by the way, was Martin Steer, who was quickly nicknamed Heifer!

One evening, whilst walking past the school chapel, the Director of Music pounced. A basket filled with music on the front of a wartime bicycle appeared out of nowhere and the chapel lamp lit up the angular and animated features and wild dark hair of the Director of Music.

"Ah Dalby, there you are!" His staccato colonial accent had been honed in Dar-es-Salaam and was always full of boyish enthusiasm.

"I hear the viola lessons are going well?"

"Yes, sir," I lied. I was and am still, an atrocious string player.

"Good! Well now that your voice has changed why don't I give you a voice trial and see if you have any singing voice."

"Er…no, thank you, sir, I really don't sing at all."

"Nonsense!" He quickly rejoined, leaning his bike against the flint wall and opening the chapel door.

The next thing I knew, I was in the dusty vestry staring down at the fingerboard of an old grand piano.

"Do you know what note this is?" He banged a white key and it sounded high. "It's D," he prompted.

"And this one?" he banged a lower note that sounded the same.

"D?" I proffered.

"Exactly! They are both the same note but an octave apart in pitch."

"Mmm." I nodded dully, anxious to leave.

"Right! The word Kyrie is a Greek word and the first part of the mass that is otherwise in Latin. Sing Keee…long like this on the high D and two short notes ri…e on the low D as loudly as you can. I'll play it with you."

"KY…RI…E!!!" I boomed at the top of my voice.

When the dust had settled and the echo in the chapel had died away, I stood with mouth open and eyes wide in astonishment. Silently and deliberately, the piano lid closed.

"And that young Dalby is the first bar of the great Mass in D minor by Joseph Haydn called the Nelson Mass. If you join the choir now, the senior boys mostly from your house, will help you learn to read music if you just follow them and sing what they sing. If you can do that, you can come on the tour to Holland at the end of term which means you miss the last week of term, exam week. Are you in?"

It was a done deal as far as I was concerned and the answer to all my troubles. This was how to avoid my Maths exam!

"Absolutely. Yes, sir!"

"Good, well done, see you after supper for choir practice, keep the score and read it and re-read it until you are completely familiar with it."

I stepped out into the close and gazed around at the medieval silhouette of the cloisters and thought to myself: *Dear God, what have I let myself in for?* I was though, rather elated, and still a bit surprised at the strong reverberation of my first vocal attempt that was, I have to say, rather empowering.

To say that the evening in the chapel vestry was a life-changing moment would be an understatement. The rest of my academic life at Dover took very much a back seat as the chapel choir and its many continental tours and cathedral performances simply took over all other concerns except, perhaps, cricket.

The first tour of Holland went extremely well with soloists made up from choral scholars from King's and St John's Cambridge and a talented parent soprano whose son (Rupert Baker) sang treble in the choir and who went on to be a bit of a star, as a fireman in ITV's *London's Burning*.

My first cathedral trip was to sing the weekend services at Coventry Cathedral. I remember standing in the choir stalls looking up at the vast crown over the quire made up of enormous thorns. I was on the Cantori's side but the other half of the choir, the Decani or Deacons side, were so far away you could hardly hear them. My whole memory of the place was a vast warehouse of nails and thorns and garish 1960s stained glass windows. The designers had given little if any thought to acoustics and the sound just evaporated into the vast space above giving no help to the singers. I, of course, blamed the Germans.

The following year, I learnt that the treble section of the choir made up of unbroken voices from the junior school in Folkestone, had recruited a most unlikely candidate, my brother John. I supposed he had joined the choir to see more of me but he said no and that it was his best friend who had persuaded him to join (presumably to get out of the end of term exams). And so it was, that two singing Dalbys set off across the channel en route for *'High Germany'* ('Germania Superior' in Latin).

We crossed the border into Germany and our coach made steady progress through the dark forests, heavily laden with snow, with our ETA slipping ever later as the snow fell ever thicker and the speed of the coach continued to reduce as the visibility deteriorated. Then a minor miracle; we pulled over at a motel and our German-speaking member of staff went in to negotiate. Incredibly, they managed to find accommodation for all 40 of us boys and staff and presumably accepted the College credit card. The hotel was cosy and to my great astonishment and joy, I discovered that I had no trouble getting served wonderful German beer after I admitted that I was only 15. The staff were too preoccupied billeting the junior choristers and the Cambridge choral scholars gave us every encouragement. The tour just kept getting better as we reached the stunning university city of Heidelberg. We were all to be billeted with charming local families so it was pot luck if you drew an ageing couple who talked about the terrible bombing (American, of course) during the war or a more entertaining younger family. I hit the jackpot without a doubt. A man in a black leather jacket stood in the crowd and called out my name "Graaaahem Daalby?"

"Ja, ja das bin ich," I yelled back, trying to show off my appalling O–level German.

"Ach zo? You speak German? Super! But all my daughters are looking forward to meeting you and practicing zher English."

"All your daughters?" I replied, eyebrows raised.

"Sure! I hef five of zem vaiting to meet you, please?" he said, gesturing to a gleaming brand-new Mercedes. We sped off through the snow-clad forests to a huge mansion of a house with several more Mercs parked outside. We entered via a marble-floored hallway and into a large drawing room that suddenly exploded into life in the form of five unfeasibly beautiful Rhine Maidens aged between 14 and 24. They were all blonde and adept at doing the formal handshaking thing whilst introducing themselves as I struggled to remember the very traditional Aryan/Norse names, Gretchen, Sigrid, Annaliese, Inge und Heidi (whilst pinching myself).

The snow fell thickly around the stunning High Baroque architecture of Heidelberg church and as I stepped out of my black Mercedes with my high-heeled escort of five Rhine Maidens, there were envious mutterings from my colleagues along the lines of "Dalby! The jammy so-and-so!" The night ended in a Bier Keller when I discovered Weizenbier (wheat beer) and the effects it can have on speech when imbibed in sufficient quantity. I think they also got me to stand on the table and sing *In München steh't ein Hoffbrauhaus* whilst swinging a stein of beer. I awoke with a heavy head and the youngest of the daughters banging on the door shouting, "You must stand up now!" ('Aufstehen' means to get up).

Chapter 5
A Really Spooky Story

Dover College Chapel – originally the pilgrims rest-house at Dover Priory

It was a dark and stormy night. No, actually, it really was! It was tipping down and I was entertaining some colleagues to tea and biscuits in my study and discussing the incredible new topic of the arrival of girls into a hitherto all-male environment excepting Cook and, of course, Matron! We were on the particular subject of whether or not they could cut the mustard in the choir as the Junior School trebles had now been displaced. It was at this moment that the head of the choir 'Choregus', in the person of Backhouse (now well-known and respected as the director of the Vasari Singers) knocked and entered with a large medieval key. Apparently, the Housemaster had complained to the Director of Music that Backhouse had not done as well as expected in his mock A-level exams due to the time spent with the choir which he must now give up for the remainder of the term. As Backhouse had come to Dover, having been Head

Chorister at Canterbury Cathedral, the choir was an important part of his life and he was not happy. He was especially not happy at being told that I, a year his junior and who, until only recently, could barely read music, was to take over with immediate effect. The only upside for him was that he would not now have to go out in the truly biblical weather to set out the music for the morning choir practice. It was suggested that I might prefer to get up early in the morning rather than risk an encounter with the grey monk, who had often been sighted slipping silently between shadowy pillars in the ancient flint and timber housing that had once served as the Priory guest room for poorer travellers seeking shelter. But a challenge had been thrown down in front of my fellow students and I couldn't back out now without losing face.

Throwing on an overcoat and clutching the huge medieval key, I left my friends in the warmth and comfort of my study to face the night. It was just a short walk from School House to the chapel door, which I reached around 10:15pm, having been duly soaked and battered by the wind. A small lamp and the lightning flashes illumined the great oaken door so that I was able to make out the gouges in the wood caused by the shrapnel from the shelling that was a constant part of Dover life from 1939. In a medieval door such as this, they were mere flesh wounds. I turned the ancient lock quite easily and put my shoulder to the heavy door and as it opened, I was aware of musty, warm air from within, tinged with an aroma of candles and incense. We were quite High Anglican in those days. Relieved to be out of the deluge, I reached for the light switch that illumined the carved-oak Quire which, at that time, had been moved away from the altar and placed at the West end of the chapel, near the organ pipes, on the orders of the Director of Music. Up at the altar, a red icon was flickering, casting an uncertain dim, religious light and the stained-glass windows further illumined the East end of the chapel. Just then, a brilliant lightning bolt bathed the whole chapel in electric blue, and my heart missed a beat or two, not for the crash of the ensuing thunder but for the fact that I could clearly make out the figure of a man in a dark cassock kneeling at the steps of the altar, partly concealed by an eleventh-century pillar. I blinked quickly and, as I broke into a cold sweat and my heartbeat moved into double-time, reason returned and I breathed heavily in relief.

"Evening, sir," I called out from some 50 paces away, "It's Dalby, I've just come to set out tomorrow's music as I've taken over from Backhouse."

There was no reply and as I didn't wish to disturb further the Chaplain's prayers (although I did wonder at such piety so late and on such a terrible night), I quickly set about laying out the psalms and the anthem for the following day. Calling out a cheery goodnight, I switched off the light at the West end and pulling the great oaken door behind me, I locked it, knowing that the Chaplain would come and go, as he always did via the vestry back door. I returned to my study to find my friends had been helping themselves to my supply of biscuits and evicted them with the news that my ordeal had not been at all creepy due to the presence of the college chaplain.

The aptly named Sunday broke with glorious autumnal sunshine, giving a golden glow to the few remaining yellow leaves that clung obstinately to the dripping boughs recovering from the previous night's deluge. The morning service went surprisingly well with the newly formed soprano section keen to prove that they were a match for the displaced boy trebles from the junior school. As I disrobed in the vestry, the chaplain came over to say how well the choir was progressing and invited me to join him with other staff members and parents for a glass of sherry at his place. This was clearly one of the perks of the job and I gladly accepted. It was here that I raised the subject of the previous evening, adding that it had been a relief to have had some company on such a stormy night in an eleventh-century building that boasted so many sightings of a monkish apparition. The chaplain frowned and said, "Oh come now, Dalby, you surely don't believe in all that nonsense do you?"

I found this odd given that the whole basis and control of the Christian Church had for two thousand years, been founded upon the fear of the Afterlife and I put this to him. He waved me away with a deprecatory gesture of the hand adding:

"In any event, my wife and I were having dinner with the Vicar of St Mary's Folkestone and didn't get back till gone eleven o'clock."

"Does anyone else have a key?" I asked suspecting the answer and feeling the small hairs on the back of my neck beginning to rise.

"Oh, just a spare for the cleaners who leave it here when they have finished, why do you ask?" I drank the sherry down in one and shuddered as I went in search of a hasty re-fill.

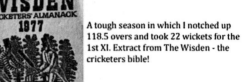

A tough season in which I notched up 118.5 overs and took 22 wickets for the 1st XI. Extract from The Wisden - the cricketers bible!

DOVER COLLEGE

Played 15: Won 2, Lost 11, Drawn 2

BATTING

	Innings		Not Outs		Runs		Highest Inns.		Average
M. C. Sloman	14	..	0	..	489	..	113	..	34.92
*R. F. McAlpin	15	..	0	..	360	..	88	..	24.00
S. J. Theobald	15	..	0	..	273	..	70	..	18.20
G. J. Dalby	11	..	1	..	139	..	35	..	13.90
W. J. Medlicott	15	..	1	..	153	..	41	..	10.92

BOWLING

	Overs		Maidens		Runs		Wickets		Average
J. Care	73	..	16	..	237	..	17	..	13.94
G. J. Dalby	118.5	..	18	..	407	..	22	..	18.50
J. M. Johnson	53.5	..	0	..	261	..	12	..	21.75
A. Haffner	103	..	25	..	309	..	13	..	23.76

Wearing my 1st XI Cricket Colours

Chapter 6
Out into the World

With unseemly haste, my blissful time at school was drawing to an end and both my father and my school tutors appeared to be concerned as to what I was intending to do with myself at the end of my final term. I could waste time doing some sort of degree in History or English but as I hadn't really put in the spadework academically, it would probably end up being in some ghastly red-brick monstrosity so nicely denounced by the Prince of Wales. No Oxford or Cambridge for me! It looked like my father's long-laid plans for me to go into the Army might well come to fruition. I had spent a number of school holidays on exercise with the CCF (Cadet Force) usually on Dartmoor or somewhere bleak and I had done various Army interviews, usually along the lines of interest that I was in the shooting, fencing and cricket teams and that I could ride a horse to an average standard. "Jolly good…we shall look forward to seeing you at Sandhurst!"

I did in fact spend a week at Sandhurst, in Alamein block if you're interested, where I was told I should join the Hussars, rather like Young Winston. I was greeted in the Mess by a tall, blond blushing figure, who I recognised immediately as Perkins, my Head of House when I had been a junior. He gushed and blushed enthusiastically about what a fabulous life it was and how marvellous it was that another Dovorian had chosen the Queen's colours. He made a wonderful recruiting officer but I was not convinced. The British Army at this time was very much confined to Aldershot, Northern Ireland, North Germany and Salisbury Plain. None of these places had much appeal for me and my mind was set upon returning to Singapore or the Far East.

It was in my final term at school with my exams almost completed that a strange quirk of fate decided that my first mode of employment should be to remain in the education system but on the other side of the desk. Drinking tea with my feet up and listening to Rossini loudly in my study one evening, I was rudely interrupted by an unexpected knock on the door.

"Come!" I yelled over the *Barber of Seville*, thinking it to be a colleague. I jumped to my feet, knocking over my chair, as the opening door revealed not only my Housemaster, but a fierce-looking man of athletic build with gold spectacles, red cheeks, blond-red hair and eyebrows, and piercing green eyes. He cut an imposing figure, filling my study. I later learnt he had played rugby for the 'Varsity', had been a Housemaster at Repton and was now the no-nonsense Headmaster of Tormore Prep School in Deal. My own Housemaster had suggested earlier that he thought I might be good at teaching and was clearly following up this line of thought. He asked me at once not to call him Sir or Mr anything. He was Hare or John to his friends and Headmaster to his staff. He was abrupt to the point of being blunt but we seemed to click instantly…

"1st XI Cricket? Impressive."

"Well, left-arm spinner and opening bat by default as the original cover-drove his Achilles heel during the first match of the season and won't be playing much this year."

"Ha! lucky for you, eh?" And slapped me hard between the shoulder blades.

"Right…here's the situation! One of my staff has sadly been called off the field (he meant he had died) and I need someone to start in September to cover for a year. He taught Latin and Greek but we have that covered. What we need is a young man to live in and look after the borders some weekends. You will need to take Football, Rugby and Cricket teams and to teach English, History, Geography and Scripture and write an end of term play for your form…can you do that?"

My Housemaster was nodding at me behind his back and I found myself joining in the nodding. "Splendid," he boomed and shook my hand vigorously. "I shall write to confirm everything and shall see you in the Michaelmas Term, one week before the boys get back…goodnight!" and off he strode.

A colleague of mine entered my study.

"Who the hell was that? We could hear him right down the corridor!"

"That was Hare, John Hare, my first employer. I'm going to be a prep school master you see?" I could hardly believe it myself. I was still just 18.

The end of term arrived and I bid a sad and fond farewell to friends and colleagues with whom I had lived cheek-by-jowl since the age of 13 when my voice was high and my cheek unshaven. With a job to return to, I spent a fabulous late summer touring Europe and pitching tents in Innsbruck, Verona, Assisi, Sienna and as far south as Naples. The world was my lobster!

A class in the old building of Tormore Prep School

Returning from that halcyon summer, I discovered that Tormore was a fine old Georgian building and that my lodgings were opposite the old church and within staggering distance of a splendid pub which I remember was called The Admiral Kepple (whoever he may have been). My position among the staff halved the average age in an instant but they all seemed relieved to have me on board to take over the sports duties that they clearly didn't relish. The master I had replaced was someone the boys were keen to tell me all about. He was just 40 but had appeared much older and was a tyrannical and unpredictable character. A Classics genius and a desperate alcoholic, he fulfilled his physician's dire presentiments as his organs gave up the unequal struggle. His name was Raven and his surviving brother was keen to meet the incoming master of so little experience (none, in fact). I was invited to join him at The Kepple by another master Michael Webb (Classics and Maths) who said that everyone called him 'The Captain' but that his name was actually Simon Raven, the celebrated author. In the mid 70s, Simon Raven was indeed something of a celebrity. He had served in Kenya as a captain and was now much sought after as a screenwriter, having had some huge successes including 'Edward and Mrs

Simpson' starring Edward Fox and 'I Claudius' starring Derek Jacobi, which remain highly regarded even today.

The Admiral Kepple was an eighteenth-century smugglers-style pub with low ceilings and lattice windows. The Captain was sitting in the back bar nursing a large gin and tonic. His demeanour was very much that of a retired colonial army officer. With his curly blond hair thinning on top and his freckled sun-beaten face, I put his age around 55. He had a wicked twinkle in his eye and the permanent expression of one who has just heard a mildly dirty joke. You would never have questioned his sexuality in a month of Sundays. Which made it all the stranger that, whenever I met the Captain from then on, he was always accompanied by a tall thin man wearing black, skin-tight leather or silk trousers, a loose-fitting white smock shirt with a frill and sporting long black ringlets in the style of the Merry Monarch. He just needed the Spaniel. He pouted and gazed at me through half-closed eyes as he appraised what he apparently suspected might be an intruder on his turf. I had never really met a full-on, out of the closet 'Gay' before but his conversation reminded me of Anthony Blanche in Brideshead Revisited in his amusing, waspish barbs, mostly directed at the headmaster's wife, who was charming. As time was called we all trudged back to the Old School House where I lived and vast bulbous glasses were produced and filled to the brim with the largest gin and tonics I had seen or have seen since. With my rapidly deteriorating powers of speech, I was about to take my leave and mount the narrow spiral staircase when the Captain suddenly turned to me and said, "You know, if I was a young man in your shoes, I think the only decent job these days would be to get a commission in a colonial police force and see the world."

I staggered upstairs and collapsed on the bed, which then took on all the attributes of a carousel, as the words "colonial police force" kept repeating in my brain.

Just a few days later, I was spending a dull Sunday afternoon marking books, when my eye fell upon a colour page of a supplement in the Times. On pulling it out, I saw that it was a full-page advertisement placed by the Hong Kong government. The photograph was of a smart young officer in black uniform, pip on shoulder, Sam Brown belt, lanyard and revolver, leaping out of a blue Land Rover with his loyal Chinese sergeant and P.C.'s behind him. 'Join the Hong Kong Police' it read, 'Apply now'. I could hardly believe the coincidence. Reaching for the port decanter that I had ordered with my first month's pay; I began to fill out the form.

It was not long before the full Hong Kong Government application arrived from Dover Street in Mayfair and shortly after, I was on a train up to London for the first of many interviews. After several months, the vast horde of applicants had been whittled down to about 30 with another ten still to be rooted out. I was beginning to get to know the other applicants by now.

One major problem standing in my path was a rather zealous and over-protective doctor in Harley Street who claimed he had sent people out to Hong Kong only to see them return a few weeks later as emotional and psychological wrecks. He had said at my medical that I was too light and was very concerned about my heart history. I added that I was very fit, played a lot of sport and that I would return after lunch for a weigh-in and I would be up to the minimum weight of nine and a half stone! "Are you sure you know what you are letting yourself in for?" he said. "I've seen men twice your size come back in pieces after a month. Those housing estates have a hundred thousand people in each block. It's a very dangerous job, you know, and you are very slightly built."

"And the Chinese aren't?" I replied giving him a steely look.

"Right!" he said. "I'll see you for weighing at 2:30 and you may keep your trousers on but not your jacket," he added with a knowing glance.

"I came out of the doctors into Harley Street and headed for Marylebone where there might be restaurants. Sure enough, a Trattoria hove into sight and I dived into the empty eatery. Buon Giorno, Signor, tayble for one?"

"Yes please…I haven't much time so can I have spaghetti meatballs to start followed by steak Milanese with sautéed potati fritti, zucchini fritti and Tiramisu to finish. Oh, and half a bottle of Montepulciano, please? I have one hour."

"Si Signor! Bravo! Raite awaiy! Eh Giovanni! Presto, presto per il signor." Munching on the breadsticks, I brooded on the fact that I had an hour and a half to add slightly over a quarter of a stone. Could I do it? I was wondering what the doctor had meant by that look as he mentioned keeping my trousers on. Then, the penny dropped, in a very literal sense.

Puffing slightly as I finished off the creamy pudding of sponge and marsala, I paid the admiring waiter and emerged into the sunlight gazing at my watch as I did so. I just had time to find a bank and hand over a twenty-pound note in exchange for several bags of coins. In Rymans, I bought a roll of tape and was back in Harley Street by 2:25. Popping into the bathroom, I quickly taped the bags up my thighs and placed one in each pocket.

"Come through please, Mr Dalby, and remove your jacket. If you would just stand on the scales."

I clanked onto the weighing scales like a medieval man-at-arms, and I saw his eyebrows rise suddenly in astonishment.

"Good lunch, was it, Mr Dalby?"

"Oh yes!" I beamed. "Very!"

"Right, well all now seems in order, you have met with the requirements of medical fitness as stipulated by the Hong Kong government and your heart operation does not appear to impede you in any way so I shall send the positive results off to your prospective employers."

"Thank you, Doctor," I said and clanked out of the surgery complete with my strap-on chain mail. Emerging from the bathroom, I noticed the patients in the waiting room looked somewhat alarmed, as did the nurse, who had been listening to the muffled screams and yelps emanating from the echoing, tiled acoustic as I removed the tape from my inner thighs.

HONG KONG GOVERNMENT OFFICE
6 GRAFTON STREET LONDON W1X 1L2

THIS IS TO CERTIFY THAT
Mr. G.J. Dalby has been appointed
as Inspector in the Royal Hong Kong
Police Force with effect from
2nd December 1977.

(F. S. McCosh)
for Commissioner

10th November 1977

Appalling typing by Government secretary confirming
my rank on my 20th Birthday and signed, for
Commissioner, by F.S. McCosh - what a name for a
Rozzer!

A few weeks later, a formal offer arrived of a commission in the Royal Hong Kong Police at the rank of Junior Inspector (2nd Lieutenant) or bomban jai (Little Inspector) as the Chinese called us. This would take effect on December 2nd, 1977, my 20th birthday, it hardly seemed possible.

The headmaster was delighted for me and asked if I might remain for the most part of the Michaelmas Term until I was due to fly which suited us both very well. I also remained at Tormore during the summer holiday as I was offered a very pleasing job teaching English to a group of visiting Spanish students who would be occupying the boys' dormitories.

It was during this time that two giants in the field of music died. The first caused a global outpouring of grief (the like of which the world was not to see until the death of Diana, Princess of Wales) and the second elicited a short obituary on about page seven of the broadsheets and no mention at all in the tabloid press. The first was Elvis Presley, with the charismatic quiff, the curling lip, the shaking leg and the arrogant swagger of one who had gone from being an illiterate truck driver to an illiterate billionaire. The second, who had died six months earlier was, begging Elgar's pardon, the greatest English composer since Henry Purcell in the person of Edward Benjamin Britten 1913–1976. The reason I mention this will become clear. I had fielded a call from Leo, the eccentric Director of Music at Dover, saying that there was to be a memorial concert at The Royal Festival Hall for Benjamin Britten and did I want to go? As just about every significant artist associated with Britten was going to be there it wasn't going to be a difficult question to answer. There would be Sir Peter Pears, Phillip Langridge, King's College Choir, the Britten Sinfonia and the horn player, Alan Civil. It was during the Serenade for Tenor, Horn and Strings and specifically during the movement entitled Dirge, a terrifying medieval poem, as Phillip Langridge was singing *and Christ receive thy soul*, when there came an awful noise from the seats in the stalls below our balcony. I peered over and saw a bevy of St John's Ambulance crew ferrying out some poor chap near the front. The concert continued unabated and I forgot about the incident until afterwards in the foyer when we bumped into my former singing teacher, the Winchester Cathedral tenor, William Kendall, who had been sat at the front near the man who was stretchered out. It transpired that as Langridge sang *and Christ receive thy soul,* this poor chap had suffered a fatal heart attack. Now that's what you call timing!

After the concert, we had been invited to a flat in Prince of Wales Drive, Battersea, to have supper with an airline pilot called George who had been at Dover and a very well-known presenter for the BBC World Service, John Touhey. A wonderful supper was had with some interesting music which although I didn't know it, was to play a very large part later in my life. The record that caught my attention was a 1930s dance band called The Savoy Orpheans. The track, *A Nightingale sang in Berkeley Square* was being sung in that perfect English style by Anne Lenner but I could never have guessed either how this particular song would feature later in my life.

Chapter 7
Return to the Orient

The month of November 1977 drew to a close and I said my farewells to the boys I had taught and to some of the older ones to whom I had been more like a big brother, being just a few years older. The parents, incredibly, showered me with gifts such as an antique gold and pearl tiepin. It was an emotional time. Simon Raven presented me with a copy of not one of his own novels but John Le Carré's *The Honourable Schoolboy* which he signed "To Graham Dalby from Simon Raven and the best of Chinese luck to you!"

I stayed at my sister Hilary's apartment near Eton on the night of December 1st and, as she worked for BA at that time, she was able to come onto the aircraft to say goodbye. What she also did was to brief the cabin crew that it was my 20th birthday and tip them the wink to look after me. I sat next to a lanky character wearing 70s pear-shaped glasses and sporting a great Che Guevara moustache but who looked absolutely terrified. We got chatting and it transpired that he was also a new recruit for the Hong Kong Police but I kept my identity quiet for a while. As the flight got underway, I was immediately brought a glass of champagne by a very pretty stewardess without ordering it and 'Cookie', as he came to be known, watched in baffled admiration at the very special treatment I seemed to be getting in economy class. Cookie regaled me with terror stories he had heard of what happens when new recruits arrive at the Police Training School (PTS). I contented myself by enjoying the attention of the crew and the flowing champagne before nodding off.

I have flown into Hong Kong on many occasions but you never forget your first landing at Kai Tak, the legendary airport that is sadly, no more. We were coming in at sunset and we first flew very sharply around some very high hills before flying so low through Kowloon that we could see people watching television in their apartments. I really thought we were going to scrape a wingtip on one of the tower blocks when suddenly, we were out over the sea again getting ever lower and lower. We were going to land in the sea without any doubt. Then, at the last second and out of nowhere, runway lights suddenly appeared 20 feet below with sea on either side of the narrow strip. The huge plane cleared the sea and dropped onto the runway with a couple of bounces before hitting reverse so violently that only our seatbelts held us in place. "Oh my God, that was unbelievable!" I yelled turning to Cookie. His face was ashen, his mouth was hanging open and his bandito moustache drooped, setting off the whole aspect of abject terror. Edvard Munch would have reached for his palette had he seen this expression of horror. "Christ!" was all that he said and I noted that his fingers gripped the armrest and that his knuckles were white.

After landing, we grouped up to discover there had been 20 of us on the flight and we were soon herded onto waiting Police minibuses (Siu-ba). We got our first real look at the neon Hades that the Chinese call Gau-Lung (Nine dragons) but what we gwei-loh's (Round-eyes) call Kowloon. Then, under the harbour tunnel to the island of Heung Gong meaning 'Fragrant Harbour'(hilarious!) or Hong Kong in gwei-loh speak. After a long drive up the rock and past the Peak, we descended into Heung-Gong-Jai meaning Little Hong Kong, which had somehow got translated as Aberdeen Harbour. And this is where PTS (Police Training School) was situated.

The initial feeling of excitement of driving through the guardhouse gave way to one of apprehension after the minibus drivers parked up outside a lit barrack block and simply disappeared, leaving us sat uneasily for what seemed an eternity and wondering what we should be doing. Suddenly, the silence was shattered and the air turned a parade ground blue as a broadside of expletives had us doubling into the barracks, clutching our suitcases, and standing to attention by a bed. All of this whilst being hotly pursued by officers in jet black uniforms sporting swagger sticks and bushy moustaches. Questions were screamed at us at point-blank range in a no-win format and the penalty was always "drop and give me 20!" (press-ups). Soon, we were issued with T-shirts, shorts and pumps. We were then taken out for an impromptu 45-minute floodlit foot-drill class on the parade ground. All those whose hair was deemed to be too long were marched off to the demon camp barber for a number one. My hair was mercifully spared as I had had the foresight to get a regulation officer-length haircut before I flew. I was finding this all hugely amusing as my birthday festivities on the flight had me still in a party mood. I was well-versed in army foot-drill so didn't get picked on for making basic mistakes, like turning the wrong way when everyone turns right, and you find yourself nose to nose with the man behind you, wondering if he had made the mistake or you. The other classic is to start marching by putting the left foot and the left arm out at the same time. I had clicked that this was merely an amusing part of the initiation ceremony and took it all in good part, unlike some of my exhausted colleagues. One slightly overweight chap, having done the best part of a hundred press-ups, could take no more and tendered his resignation after only an hour. He was ushered away never to be seen again. Finally, at around 11:00 local time, we were marched over to a darkened building with silhouetted palm trees and some sort of duck in a cage outside. There we stood in our shorts in the darkness as a light rain began to fall. *What now? I thought.*

"Christ!" said a voice. I hadn't noticed that Cookie was on my right, almost unrecognisable without his long hair and glasses but for the moustache that caught the rain. On my left was a tall, lean, hard-looking Scotsman who had caught the interest of Heathrow security when they discovered a cut-throat razor in his hand luggage.

A voice barked, "You! What's your name?"

"MacKay, sir,"

"Well, Mackay, can you sing?"

"No, sir!"

"Well, that's a bloody shame seeing as it's nearly Christmas! Sing me a carol or I'll have the lot of you standing out here till it is Christmas!"

"I cannae sing sur and tha's the trewth of it." MacKay was digging his heels in. Time to step in here, I thought, as I was probably the only one in the squad with that particular skill. Out of the corner of my mouth, I told him to follow my lead. In the darkness, they might not notice that it wasn't him. *Oh come all ye faithful…*I boomed in my choir-trained baritone voice. MacKay did follow me and his cracked, mono-tonal version sung in a broad Isle of Skye accent confirmed that he had, indeed, been telling the truth. I began laughing uncontrollably but fortunately for me, the other officers were busy encouraging the others to join in with the polite exhortation of "Sing you bastards!" so I was spared another 20 press-ups. At the end of the first verse, the ad hoc chorus faltered and I did not offer any further assistance as I was still incapacitated by mirth at the expense of poor MacKay's viva voce. Silence fell and blinking the tears from my eyes, I was aware that we were alone once more. A voice called out in the middle distance:

"Can you take a joke?"

"Oh Christ!" said Cookie, now appointed the official squad blasphemer. There was a general worried murmur of assent from our ranks.

"I said can you take a joke?" the voice repeated, louder and with a hint of menace.

"Yes, sir!" we yelled in unison.

At this point, the whole world exploded into a bank of floodlights and flashing cameras and we realised that we had been standing outside the Officers Mess with the entire camp's trainee officer corps waiting silently in the darkness for us to finish our ordeal of humiliation. Silver trays of beer were waiting and we were herded into the Mess by laughing and smiling faces. At last, our ordeal was over. Or so we thought…

After several/many very welcome pints of Philippines brewed San Miguel, we were invited to get suited up once more as we were told that a special trip to 'The Wanch' had been organised to celebrate our arrival and that it was compulsory and traditional. To the question of "what's the Wanch?" came a roar of laughter and knowing looks from the other officers. A convoy of red taxis had appeared from nowhere and we all piled in and headed off back the way we had come over the gap and down into the district known as Wanchai and specifically, into Lockhart Road. This whole street was brightly illumined with neon signs advertising every type of bar with names such as 'Bottoms Up', 'The Hot Lips Club', 'The Butterfly Club' and 'The Suzie Wong'. It was just 17 years since the film *Suzie Wong* was made and how dated that now looks. Not much had changed by 1977. We split up into smaller groups of four or five with an officer from the senior intakes acting as host. None of us had had a chance to change any currency as we swept past a heavy curtain into one of the purple-lit bars. We were greeted by a gold-toothed mamma-san of middle years wearing a fetching silk emerald green cheung-saam, buttoned to the neck.

"OK, listen up guys…we have set up a tab for you, which should cover you for three or four gin and tonics and a couple of drinks for the girls but when that runs out you're on your own. Don't give the girls any money! Your task is to find your way back to PTS by morning. Good luck!"

With that, he disappeared out into the bright neon street. I was quickly joined by a doll-like Chinese girl who I was surprised to see was naked from the waist upward. She carried this off so gracefully that after a few minutes this seemed perfectly natural. Before long my three other colleagues had drifted off into the street probably from sheer exhaustion and a sensible plan to stick together in their efforts to get back home to the PTS barracks over the other side of the island. I, however, was too captivated by my new young friend whose atrocious English didn't stop her chatting and giggling at everything. She had nick-named me something in Cantonese which she translated as "velly handsome chelly boy" which made the other girls dissolve into giggles but as to the meaning, I had absolutely no idea. When I had finally had enough of gin and tonics and delightful female company and as it was gone 2:00 a.m., I thought it wisest to attempt to get back to PTS before the alcohol and exhaustion really kicked in. Before I left, I was made to promise to return with "Eeb Sam Oron" which left me baffled as I had never even met him until one of the girls showed me an empty bottle of Yves Saint Lauren perfume! Ah!

After some difficulty in getting a taxi, I managed to get one to accept UK money, as the 50 pence piece was exactly the same shape and size as a five-dollar coin and he seemed happy to take four of these which I found very gratifying.

The next problem was trying to get him to understand where I wanted to go. Finally, something I said made him understand:

"Aaaah! PeeeTeeeeEssseeee?" he asked. I nodded and off we went with Cantonese radio blaring and the bizarre thing was that every now and then, I could catch the English word 'gin and tonic' amidst the rapid-fire local Cantonese dialect. After the great climb up and down the mountain, we arrived on the other side of the island at almost 3:00 a.m. and I was decanted from the red taxi. To my great surprise and consternation, a black-uniformed PC slammed to attention and saluted at the guardhouse with the greeting:

"Good Eeebelling, sir!"

I managed a lazy salute back, despite not being in uniform or wearing a hat, which are the two prerequisites. He checked my passport, and the barrier was raised. I sincerely hope he didn't turn around to watch me after that as just 30 yards later, I encountered a steep grassy slope to the right of the pavement which, for some reason, I found myself rolling down until I came to rest at the bottom where I recognised the parade ground from earlier in the evening. This unplanned and unexpected shortcut had given me the landmark I needed to locate my barrack block, which I reached, to discover that quite a number of my colleagues had not yet made it back. I fell into a dreamless coma after a 48-hour marathon.

I awoke at around midday on a hot Sunday and gazed around the room, which contained two empty beds and a large muscular body in the fourth. There was no door but a long corridor, which contained other life forms and a deal of snoring. Just then I heard a sound so familiar, yet unfamiliar, given that it was December. It was the unmistakable sound of leather on willow. Blinking in the bright sunshine, I saw with delight, a body of some 15 white-flannelled individuals observing a shiny red ball racing to the boundary with a mild lack of interest. The ball was finally fielded, after four runs were signalled by an aged coolie in a round, pointed straw hat who threw it back underarm to one of the unenergetic fielders for play to resume once more. This was real old British Empire stuff more like 1877. I smiled to myself. Just then I felt a giant paw on my shoulder and turned to see the huge frame and grinning square jaw of my roommate. His name was David Nock but was quickly nicknamed 'Bam Bam' after the 'Flintstones' cartoon baby, on account of his being the youngest and easily the strongest in our squad.

My training with the RHKP was very time consuming and often very manual-learningly boring and my mind was often more focused on more intellectual pursuits. I squandered my salary on anything and everything from a motorbike to a hi-fi with a stack of classical records. I also bought a violin, which I would play in the barracks to the consternation of my fellow officers. One morning, whilst dressing for parade, I caught an advert on the classical radio station, RTHK, calling for singers to come and audition for a performance of Messiah. I turned up at the Cathedral hall one evening with a score and sang *Why Do The Nations So Furiously Rage Together?* to them by way of an audition. This is a fiercely fast and difficult bass aria and they were astounded that a young Gwai-loh Copper could have the ability to even attempt it. I was given an apology that all the soloists had been already booked but would I consider singing with them in the chorus. I replied that that was what I had come for. I was astonished when they, there and then, offered me the part of Jesus in the Easter performance of the Bach St Matthew Passion. It was to be performed in German with the Hong Kong Philharmonic Orchestra with a Good Friday performance in the Cathedral and a live broadcast on RTHK from the City Concert Hall (Dai Wooi Tong) on Easter Sunday. This was just amazing and could never have happened to me back in the UK.

The reality of my job struck home just before Christmas. The two empty beds in my barracks were occupied on the first Monday by two Chinese officers. One was a 40-something ex-sergeant who had worked his way up through the ranks and had scant regard for me, aged 20 and Bam-bam, aged 19. The other was a tall, good-looking Chinese lad who had served just two years as a PC before taking his officer exams that required a high standard of written English. I quickly learnt that there were many violent and unpleasant things happening in Hong Kong and the local mafia, known as The Triads, were into every form of criminal activity based around drugs and extortion. Our young Chinese colleague had fallen foul of these people whilst a PC on the beat. His body was discovered in the harbour and before I had served a month, I had attended my first Chinese funeral.

Dave Nock (Bam-Bam), Cookie, Anne Patton, Me and my sister Hilary –
Mandarin Hotel 1978

Christmas came and went and the police training became a heavy schedule of Law, Cantonese, firearms and foot-drill. At weekends, I would take off into the country on my motorbike to discover the more obscure and incredibly beautiful parts of Hong Kong and the New Territories. My sister took advantage of her job perks to fly out for a visit, and by way of entertainment, I took her and some fellow officers to 'The Mandarin' for dinner and cabaret, which was the West End cast of a show called *Oh Coward*, based on the songs and plays of Sir Noël Coward. This had a tremendous impact on me, so much so, that many years later I recorded an album of Coward songs, having learnt them by heart and performed them all around Mayfair.

With the arrival of Easter also came my first performance on a professional level. The St Matthew Passion is a work of genius by JS Bach. It is scored for double chorus and orchestra, four soloists and a further bass voice to sing the character of Jesus or Christus as it is written. The Good Friday performance in the Cathedral was just with organ but on Easter Sunday, we had the fabulous Hong Kong Philharmonic and a packed 2,000 seat concert hall and a live radio broadcast. I wore a brand-new dinner suit, hand-tailored in Kowloon, and with my very short hair and boyish looks, I couldn't have looked anything less like Jesus Christ. But my voice coach had done her work well and every night in my barracks instead of reading law manuals I would listen through headphones to a recording of Dietrich Fischer-Dieskau performing the part. I later heard the recording of the concert made by RTHK and, I must admit, that my German, intonation and the controlled power of the Passion were all there. I surprised myself, it wasn't at all bad, so much so that it came back to bite me!

It was a few days later that I was summoned to have a chat with one of the senior instructors who gave me the glad tidings that my recent law exam had been a failure. He pointed out that, as a well-reasoned piece of prose, it was an interesting read but penned by an author who had clearly not opened a police law manual for many months. Now came the bombshell. Apparently, unbeknown to me, the Commandant of PTS, who was a keen connoisseur of classical music, had been in the audience for the Bach and had noticed a very young soloist singing the part of Christus. On consulting the programme notes, it clearly stated that the baritone singing Jesus was a serving officer in the Royal Hong Kong Police.

The deal that was put to me was an interesting one. By not achieving the required mark in the law exams, I would be given the opportunity to 'back-squad', that is to say, do the last three months of the course again. The Commandant, flying in the face of Government investment in my training to date, had the most extraordinary proposal.

"What you have, young Dalby is a talent that should be pursued. Any idiot can memorise a police manual but what you have is wasted here. If you don't wish to back-squad, I can offer you an honourable discharge, a small gratuity and an open air-ticket home."

"What do I need to do for that?" I blinked in astonishment.

"I suggest you go to London, get your voice professionally trained and do something useful with it. We can't afford singing policemen here."

"Thank you, sir." I came smartly to attention, saluted and marched out of the office with much to ponder upon.

I returned to my room in the Mess and gazed at the immaculately pressed black uniform we wore in the colder months before the famous long khaki shorts spared us the discomfort of Hong Kong humidity. I walked over to the record player that had a disc of 'The Marriage of Figaro' on the turntable. I watched as the clunky mechanism moved the arm and stylus onto the gleaming vinyl and waited, past the rushing noise and the clicks, to hear the familiar Overture and the rapid semiquavers of the first few bars. I was interrupted, almost at once by a loud bang on the door and a familiar voice.

"Hey, Pang-Yau!" The door opened to reveal the huge silhouette of my erstwhile barrack-room chum Bam Bam who always addressed me by the Cantonese word simply meaning 'Mate'.

"What's up?" I yelled turning the Mozart down to merely deafening.

"I'm cashiered!" he said. "Going home. I can't believe I failed the Cantonese exam twice. I'm going back to join the Met where I won't have to learn this impossible language."

I told him my story.

"Hey that's amazing! We can go on a bit of a world trip together. We can stop anywhere as long as we keep heading West, apparently."

And so it was decided upon that, with the money and the free air travel, we should go to Thailand, India and Italy before returning home.

Chapter 8
Bangkok and Mistaken Identity

Me with an even bigger snake somewhere in Thailand!

Departing from Kai Tak airport, all the lads came to see me off and a gang of beer was consumed before saying farewell to a great bunch of boys. Bam Bam wasn't due to join me for another 24 hours so I was on my own on the first leg of my journey home. First stop, Thailand. I arrived at about 10:00 p.m. and asked a taxi to take me to a half-decent hotel in the centre of Bangkok. Given the rowdy and boozy send-off at Kai Tak, I was keen to get an early night.

I awoke to a glorious morning in good time for breakfast, showered and made my way down to the dining room. It was crowded and I sat at the one remaining empty table where the waiter immediately took my order and tottered off to fetch the fixings. A sharp clacking noise attracted my attention and I looked up to see an elegantly dressed lady enter in very high heels, slung handbag and very long gleaming jet-black hair. I was thinking that she was rather dolled up so early on, what was looking to become, a very hot day. She paused and scanned the dining area for an empty table and her eyes came to rest at the three empty chairs at my table. Her long, straight legs were much accentuated by the heels and the black pencil skirt, and she wafted over to my table with a lazy blink of fake eyelashes and a haze of perfume.

"Would you mind?" came the inevitable question in a husky, smoker's voice with an American-Thai intonation.

"Not at all," I said, half rising with a touch of the old school preux-chevalier. She draped herself, languidly, over the chair and took out a cigarette holder and fitted it with a mauve cigarette with a gold filter.

"Do you mind if I smoke?" she asked, again with a lazy batting of the long eyelashes.

"Not at all," I lied but having observed this elaborate ritual with the ebony holder, it would have taken more resolve than mine to have refused her. Something was distracting my mesmerised focus through the cloud of French perfume and Balkan tobacco to a figure directly behind her at the bar. Glancing over her shoulder, I was surprised to see the waiter performing what appeared to be some sort of local dance, which entailed him waving his arms about a good deal and continually pointing to his throat. I made a grimace of non-comprehension, so he changed his routine and began pointing frantically to the lady's back. *Had she dropped a necklace or something?* I thought. Then, all at once, my expression of confusion turned rapidly into an expression of abject incredulity. It was with profound shock that my slightly hung-over eyeballs struggled to cope with all this rapid re-focusing and now alighted to where a necklace might have been worn. The scarlet velvet choker she was wearing was simply unequal to the task of concealing the unmistakable bulge of an Adam's Apple, confirming that the lady at my table was no Adam's Spare Rib! I excused myself quickly and went up to the waiter; his head nodding frantically like one of those strange toy dogs people put in the back of their cars. My face was simply agog! But my composure and my return to the table happened almost at once and I took my seat.

"I'm most awfully sorry," I said, feigning regret, "I've just learnt that my wife and two children will be joining me shortly."

The heavily pencilled eyebrows rose in surprise and the lazy eyelids closed for a second. "My dear," she wheezed in a low counter-tenor voice, "you simply don't look old enough…such a pity, I thought we were going to get on so well."

And with that, she/he stubbed out the Sobranie cigarette and shimmered out with a clacking of stilettos and a haze of fragrance. There followed a pause so pregnant I thought it must be twins. The silence was shattered by a simultaneous explosion of guffaws and unconfined laughter, the waiters slapping each other and one waiter dropping a metal tray to complete the carnival effect. I grinned back sheepishly, feeling the heat of my red face. Here was I, Man of the World and I had just been comprehensively clean bowled by a Bangkok Ladyboy.

The following day Bam Bam arrived and, you know, I am not quite sure if I told him the story of my first breakfast in Bangkok. I would never have heard the end of it. Instead, we enjoyed ourselves in innocent tourist spots such as the Floating Market and the beautiful Thai dancers (real ladies this time) and the elephants of The Rose Garden. Slightly more laddish was the Thai boxing and the crocodile wrestling with quite a number of chaps with missing limbs holding out begging bowls and signs reading "ex-crocodile wrestler!" I befriended a young Thai student, with the lovely name of Puntip, who was studying English. Just recently, she contacted me for the first time in 40 years via Facebook to say that it was I who had inspired her to read English Literature and that she still had the complete works of Shakespeare that I gave her when I left. It lives in her office at the University of Bangkok where she is Head of English. Very humbling to think I could have helped shape someone's future like that, well, I and Will the Bard, don't you know?

For several weeks, we lived the high life until we realised with horror that we were starting to run low on funds. Missing out India altogether, we soon found ourselves eating pizza on the streets of Rome in the realisation that we couldn't afford Italian hotel prices for long. Accordingly, we returned to London and said our farewells. I went off to do my thing and we lost contact until several years later. I was in Shaftsbury Avenue, having just been to the theatre, when something seemed to kick-off towards Soho's 'China Town'. Police appeared from everywhere with much wailing of sirens and flashing of blue lights. Just then a police motorbike, a great BMW thing, roared up to me, mounted by a wapping great rozzer. He removed his helmet to reveal a rock-like square jaw grinning profusely and with the unforgettable words:

"Pang Yau! Ho ma?" (How are you, my friend?) Bam Bam had made it into the Met.

Chapter 9
A Spratt to Catch a Mackerel

Returning home to England after the fabulous lifestyle of the Far East was a bit of a shock. What? Do my own washing and cooking? absurd! But, like all disillusioned and spoilt ex-pats, I had to adjust. My sister Hilary was kind enough to let me stay at her apartment in Putney while she was off flying around the world with British Airways. Whilst re-calibrating my life, I decided to join the local Putney Choral Society. Being young and very pushy I completed just one rehearsal, at the end of which, I approached the conductor to ask who was doing the solo parts in the appointed work, Stabat Mater by Rossini. Somewhat taken aback, he shook his head and laughed. "Oh no, my dear chap! Of course, we get professional singers in to do that. It's Rossini, for heaven's sake! Operatic! You cannot expect amateur choral society voices to get over a seventy-piece orchestra even if they did have the technique. We have a tenor from the chorus of The Royal Opera House already booked."

I bridled, "May I try for the bass-baritone solo if it's not already taken?"

Now it happened, that as soon as I applied to join Putney Choral Society, I rushed out to buy a record of the piece they were performing. The Stabat Mater by Rossini is a huge operatic piece with solos more like early Verdi Bel Canto than a deeply religious piece of a mother weeping at the foot of the cross as set by Pergolesi. Have I lost you? Anyway, suffice it to say that the Bass aria was a full-blooded operatic showcase that I couldn't wait to learn. By the time I appeared at the first rehearsal with all the smart ladies from Putney whispering to each other as to who this slim, sun-tanned young man with a colonial swagger could possibly be, I had the main aria learnt and perfected. The conductor sat at the piano after the rehearsal.

"Do you *honestly* think you can manage this?" he asked me, with a good deal of incredulity infused into his intonation.

"Well, it can't hurt for you to give me a chance and then you can make up your mind."

Five minutes later, he was looking at me with a rather different expression.

"Well, we can't pay you much, I mean it's not as if you are known or anything."

"Oh, you needn't worry about that. I need the exposure. I'll do a good job for you, and it'll save the society a Covent Garden-sized fee, which I am, sure will delight the finance committee."

We shook on the deal for a very modest fee.

"Well, I thought. It's a start. A sprat to catch a mackerel."

The concert was at St Anne's Church, Wandsworth. It was a magnificent old 'Pepper Pot' church like many others built to commemorate the Battle of Waterloo in 1815. Most, like this one, dated from around 1820. The programme was a choral concert of works by Rossini and Verdi. The Verdi was the Quatro Pezzi Sacrae (Four Sacred Pieces), a work for a capella voices so the orchestra and soloists were only needed for the first half. The feeling of being in front of a large orchestra again was a thrilling reminder of my first solo concert in Hong Kong and why I had left a very good job out there. My solos went off with all the assurance and passion of someone who is desperately keen to do this for a career. The tenor ducked out of the well-known and fabulously high top Db at the end of his aria, which was disappointing. I had heard Pavarotti on my recording hit this incredibly high note and I was looking forward to this pro showing the amateurs how it was done. But I forgive him everything for what transpired next…

We were in the vestry as the chorus was going on for the second half and the tenor was just slipping on his overcoat and clutching a cheque which I glanced at enviously.

"Nice working with you," he said, "where are you singing at the moment?"

"Well, er, I'm not actually singing anywhere at present. Just back from Hong Kong and on the lookout for any singing work going."

"Well, why don't you give Covent Garden a call and mention that we sang together in the Rossini. I'm pretty sure they have auditions coming up soon."

"Thanks!" I said. "I'll be sure to do that."

Incredible to think that, at that time, such was the confidence of youth that I thought nothing of presenting myself, an untrained singer with absolutely no opera experience, not even a singing teacher, to one of the most famous opera houses in the world.

To make ends meet, I had got myself a job in Bond Street. It was the best job in the world. I worked in the classical record department of Chappell's. All I had to do all day was speak to people about new releases, different artists and conductors and advise them about classical music. I didn't even have to handle any money. In this most fashionable street, I found myself chatting amiably about music to people as varied as James Galway, John Cleese and even Barbara Cartland! Chappell's was staffed at the time with many highly knowledgeable musicians and musicologists, some retired, some just starting out. When word got out that I was auditioning to the Royal Opera House, it was all hands to the pump. Once the doors had closed on the well-heeled shoppers of Bond Street, I would go downstairs to the piano department, where a fine accompanist would be waiting, along with an ex- Welsh National Opera tenor from the hire-department, and several opera enthusiasts from sheet music. It seemed to me during those sessions that everyone was a voice-coach, but I relished their support and criticism.

And so it was that, armed with two borrowed scores from Chappell's, I found myself in the magnificent surroundings of the Crush Bar of The Royal Opera House awaiting my turn amongst a host of singers from other opera houses around the world. I sang the big Act IV aria *Pieta Rispeto Onore* from Verdi's *Macbeth* and then the more manageable Mozart ditty *Ein Mädchen oder Weibchen* from *The Magic Flute*. Looking back now, I still find it incredible that the three-man committee did not shout out "Yes, thank you very much...next!" after the first ten bars. But they listened attentively throughout and there was a pause.

"I'm afraid we haven't got any notes on you here, where are you currently singing?"

"I'm sorry?"

"Which opera house have you come from or where have you sung before?"

"Well, err, well none yet exactly although I did sing a concert with one of your tenors a few weeks ago…Rossini's Stabat Mater."

One of the committee peered over his half-moon spectacles with a doubtful expression. "Indeed? So, who is your singing teacher or vocal coach?"

"Ah, well…I'm working in Chappell's of Bond Street and there's a pianist there and a retired Welsh National tenor who have been helping me."

I think I caught a twitch of a smile but the three remained benignly inscrutable.

"Thank you, Mr Dalby, we'll be in touch, thank you for coming…"

I hastened down the curved staircase to the foyer, desperate to get into the fresh air.

When I returned to Chappell's, there was a sort of hero's-welcome and they wanted to hear every detail. I thought for a moment:

You know I used to play cricket for the Hong Kong Police? Well, imagine if I had written to the MCC and told them I had just returned and was letting them know that I was available for selection for the upcoming tour against the West Indies.

That was just a little of how short I felt I had come to being offered a position in this Mecca of the opera world.

A week later, a small white envelope plopped onto the doormat with a red ROH logo stamped on it. I pulled the letter out carefully and the typed message read as expected:

Dear Mr Dalby,

Thank you for coming to sing to us recently. I'm afraid that it is not possible to offer you a position here at the moment. We feel that your voice is not yet ready to undertake the amount of singing required in chorus work and that you may harm your voice if you do this kind of singing at your age…

I put the letter down with a deep sigh of disappointment knowing, of course, that every word was true and quietly impressed at the constructive tone. I did not read on.

It was about an hour later that I picked up the letter to put it back in its envelope when I noticed that it continued with a more positive…

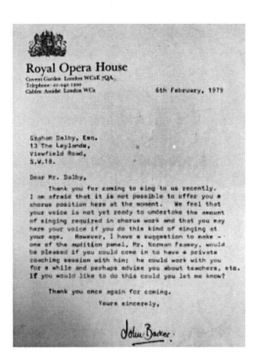

Royal Opera House
Covent Garden, London WC2E 7QA.
Telephone: 01-240 1200
Cables: Aroside London WC2

6th February, 1979

Graham Dalby, Esq.
13 The Leylands,
Viewfield Road,
S.W.18.

Dear Mr. Dalby,

Thank you for coming to sing to us recently.
I am afraid that it is not possible to offer you a
chorus position here at the moment. We feel that
your voice is not yet ready to undertake the amount
of singing required in chorus work and that you may
harm your voice if you do this kind of singing at
your age. However, I have a suggestion to make -
one of the audition panel, Mr. Norman Feasey, would
be pleased if you could come in to have a private
coaching session with him; he could work with you
for a while and perhaps advise you about teachers, etc.
If you would like to do this could you let me know?

Thank you once again for coming.

Yours sincerely,

John Barker.

"However, I have a suggestion to make, one of the audition panel, Mr Norman Feasey, would be pleased if you could come in to have a private coaching session with him…

It took several re-readings to get my head around this unexpected appendix. So, not only were they taking my audition seriously, but here I was, being offered a leg-up by the Royal Opera House and some sessions with one of the world's most eminent voice coaches; a man who regularly worked with some of the greatest singers around at that time.

A week later, I was back in ROH, backstage this time, in amongst hordes of ballerinas flitting to and fro and large bits of scenery being moved. I stood spellbound, as Norman Feasey corrected my performance of the Count's aria from the Marriage of Figaro.

"Remember the Count is an aristocrat with supreme authority. Your voice must convey that without sounding angry. The outrage he feels is in the music that Mozart has written. Mozart knew all about outraged aristocrats and his phrases will convey the force of your authority if you will allow them to."

I could have listened to him all day but as the banging of the carpenters grew, he closed the piano lid and said, "Right, I've had a word with a friend of mine who I think would be very good for you. Her name is Elizabeth Hawes, a highly regarded singing teacher, here is her number, she is expecting your call." It transpired that 'Libby' as she was affectionately known, was head of the singing faculty at Trinity College of Music. After a few lessons with her and a recital with her other students, she began to think the impossible.

One morning after a lesson, she looked up from the piano and asked me if I could play an instrument to any standard. When I told her that I had once massacred a Handel Violin Sonata at a concert in Dover (with harpsichord and 'cellist desperately trying to make me sound better), her face lit up. It appears that she had been making some discreet enquiries at Trinity but the main objection to getting into a music college in those days was at least an A level in music, plus two others, grade five theory, grade eight first study and grade six or over for second study instrument. I had A levels but nothing whatsoever in music, not even grade one triangle. It was then with some astonishment that I found myself preparing for an audition at this great music conservatoire in the august and benign presence of the conductor and Principal, Meredith Davies. Leo came up from Dover to accompany me on the piano and the panel listened as I sang my programme: *Sea Fever* by John Ireland, *Ich Grolle Nicht* by Robert Schumann and *The Count's Aria* from Le Nozze di Figaro by Mozart as taught to me by Covent Garden's senior coach. The crunch came when I had to play my second study piece and my bow started shaking as I attempted the

The Entrance Hall at Trinity College of Music

Meditation from Thais by Massenet. Mercifully, Meredith waved me to stop after just a few bars. "Yes, yes, I think we've heard quite enough of that!" he said with a genial smile. I laid my violin on the piano lid and was aware of a steely look over half-moon spectacles being levelled at me by the Academic Registrar. He looked just like the Kapellmeister in the film *Amadeus* and was eying me with a great deal of misgiving.

"What key is that?" he asked stabbing a boney finger at the three sharps on the page.

"A major, of course!" I replied, trying to look offended.

"And if they were flats?" he snapped, not giving up so easily.

"Well, E flat major; the key Beethoven chose for his third Symphony 'Eroica' opus 55. I know the score well."

I had hoped I hadn't overplayed my hand but Meredith was suppressing his amusement as the Academic Registrar glowered. I remember his name was Cyril Cork and he made it clear, that he really didn't like me.

It was early summer when a letter arrived for me with the TCM logo on it and I opened it with trembling fingers. There seemed a lot of pages for a rejection letter. I took it out slowly to read the first line of "we regret that on this occasion…" But there, before my eyes, was the first line "we are delighted to be able to offer you a place…" I ripped out the document from its envelope and read and re-read the letter of acceptance. It was impossible but true. I was to spend the next four years training and studying with like-minded people to become a full-time professional musician.

Whilst studying with Libby, one of her advanced students, a Belfast tenor called George (who was in his third year at Trinity), had told me about an opera company doing an unpaid tour of a new English translation of Anna Bolena by Donizetti and one of the venues was the concert hall at Trinity. Meredith's secretary had been in the audience when I sang the smallish role of Lord Rochford, the unfortunate brother of Anne Boleyn, who gets chopped along with Smeaton, the lutenist and the rest. Apparently, she (the secretary) had told the principal that George had discovered a promising young baritone who was auditioning for Trinity and to look out for me. It seemed that Fortune was still with me then!

Chapter 10
ET in Arcadia Ego
(Trinity College of Music)

That Halcyon summer seemed to go on forever in the blissful knowledge of what September would bring. I had joined The Philharmonia Chorus as George, ever looking after me, had told me that this very fine amateur chorus was looking for student first study singers to go to Orange in France. It was an all-expenses paid trip to sing *Turandot* in the fabulous open-air first-century Roman Amphitheatre, conducted by the great Lamberto Gardelli. My favourite soprano, Theresa Zylis-Gara was singing *Liu* and Nicolo Martinucci sang *Calaf* (Nessun Dorma). I can't remember who sang *Turandot* but she was huge and dwarfed the diminutive tenor who, even in his raised shoes, still only reached her copious bosom, making their final love duet ridiculous, before the chorus came in to put them out of their misery. There were about 12 music students among the mostly older chorus and we had great fun fooling around the hotel pool or chatting in cafés during the long, warm afternoons. We only rehearsed in the evenings as it was quite South near Avignon, and too hot during the day. The evening rehearsals were divided by a delicious dinner at the Restaurant Municipale where carafes of red wine flowed before the food arrived. For some reason, the second half of the rehearsal was always full of hilarity and high jinks which our Hungarian producer took in good part. He would speak to Zylis-Gara in her native Hungarian, to Martinucci in Italian, to Gardelli's orchestra in French, to Turandot in German and to us in English without breaking stride. He was incredible. After several weeks, the production was ready to go and we did a week of sell-out performances under the stars.

When it was time to depart, I left my colleagues to fly home whilst I caught a train for a long journey to Northern Italy. I had arranged to hook up with Leo who was heading back to England via Verona. The journey seemed to take forever and when I finally arrived, I was keen to head off to the Trattoria I knew, near the great Roman Arena. It was packed and after waiting for an age to get a table, it seemed impossible to catch the waiter's eye as we were, I suppose, regarded as insignificant tourists. Just then a vast and very familiar figure entered with an entourage and was immediately surrounded by several fawning waiters. "Maestro!" I yelled, jumping up. It was none other than Gardelli himself. He must have flown in. For a moment, he looked confused and then I realised that the last time he had seen me, a few days before, I had been dressed up as a bloodthirsty Pekinese peasant delighting in the severed head of the Prince of Persia! "Scusi, Maestro sono un cantante Inglese con il coro Philharmonia per l'opera Turandot in Orange!" His eyes widened despite my dreadful Italian.

Arena di Verona

"Incredibile!" He shook my hand warmly and rattled off a load of praise regarding the standard of the chorus singing in Orange. His hand dived into his coat pocket and when it reappeared, it contained a bunch of tickets and he handed a couple to me. They were for the Arena for the following night where they were also performing Turandot that he was conducting. After that, the waiter service improved immeasurably!

Sitting in the great Arena di Verona, under the stars, the performance was delayed by a few spots of rain. During this time, vendors yelled their wares, "Panini! Candelini!"

Well, I knew what a panini was but a candelini? I waved at one of the lads and he came over and sold me a couple of birthday cake candles! I hadn't a clue what to make of this. Then, a member of the audience got up and performed a rendition of the tenor aria *Una furtiva e lagrima* to the roars and cheers of the appreciative audience. Very good it was too. I forgot about the candles and began to wonder what this must have been like when it was first built. It was completed around the time of Christ's crucifixion and could be used for gladiatorial combat or flooded for water battles. It could seat 30,000 spectators. The central area was discovered to be very fertile for growing vegetables during the Middle Ages, probably because of the quantity of blood that had seeped into its soil. During the opening games alone, thousands of slaves who had helped build this edifice were slaughtered as a sacrifice to the gods. It is the third-largest amphitheatre in the world after the Coliseum in Rome and the Amphitheatre of Padua but the only one still providing entertainment to 20,000 spectators a night during the opera festival. I was brought out of my rêverie by an announcement saying the performance would commence in ten minutes as the threat of rain had now passed. Warily, double bass players began to emerge with their huge instruments, looking up at the night sky for any hint of rain. There was none and the vast orchestra took their places in the orchestra pit. I counted 14 double basses, to give you an idea of the size of the orchestra. Then an extraordinary thing happened. 20,000 people began lighting the little candles and I followed suit. I found myself sitting in the middle of the largest birthday cake in the world in one of the most breath-taking spectacles I have ever witnessed. Then a huge crash of oriental flavoured Puccini orchestration and we were straight onto the streets of Peking for the execution of the unfortunate Prince of Persia.

I returned to England and prepared to start my new life as a university student at Trinity College, London. Yet again, I got lucky as the two friends I had made who introduced me to 1930's dance bands, John, the BBC presenter and George, the airline pilot, invited me to house-sit their Battersea flat during my first term as they were both away. It was a simple bus ride over the Albert Bridge to Oxford Street to alight at Selfridges and a short walk to the college. On the first day, all the freshers were queuing up to register and I found myself behind a fresh-faced blond lad wearing a blazer and carrying a rolled-up umbrella. He turned around with a winning smile and, extending his hand, announced his name was Andy and that he was a tenor, had been at Haileybury, and he was studying with Libby Hawes. I replied with my name, that I was a baritone and that I was also studying with…then I realised that I too was wearing a blazer and carrying a rolled-up umbrella. We stood out like Tweedle Dum and Tweedle Dee and we did in fact become inseparable friends from then on. At that moment, the Principal's secretary walked up to me and asked me if I was Graham Dalby. When I replied in the affirmative, she said, "I just wanted to make sure as the last time I saw you, you were in doublet and hose having just incurred the wrath of Henry VIII. Right, well our best baritone was an American called Biff and we have just been informed that he isn't coming back as he has been offered a contract in the States. Would you like to take his part in a concert to sing the bass duet of Purcell's Ode to St Cecilia with Jonathan Robarts?" I had heard of him and he was very good; an ex King's Cambridge choral scholar.

"Oh, so it's not a Trinity concert then?"

"No, it's a professional engagement, they are paying £50.00; it's just one duet for two bass voices with orchestra. Is that alright?"

"Oh yes indeed!" I said beaming. 50 quid and I had not even registered yet!!

I turned around and saw my new tenor friend Andy looking at me with astonishment. In 1980, 50 pounds was a fairly decent sum at a time when a pint of beer was 75p.

"How the hell did you get that?" he said laughing. I shrugged.

"Come on, let's get this registration nonsense over and check out that place up the road, it's called the Angel Tavern and it sells Samuel Smith's beer!"

The Angel Tavern became a sort of student common room for the next four years and was frequented by students and staff alike. It was conspicuous on busy days by note of having a number of 'cello cases parked outside and inside a great pile of instrument cases including violin, tuba, French horn and trumpets. Without this pub, it would not have been possible to have made friends with so many musicians who were not singers. But, even here, the singers sat together, the string players sat together, the woodwind sat together and the brass sat together. It was to my great advantage that, being a little older and with a little more experience of the world through travel, I was able to interact easily with these cliques and being of a gregarious, sociable nature, befriended many who would become the core of the orchestra that I formed the following year.

The first term passed off happily with luck and coincidence yet again playing its part. What should the set choral piece be? The Nelson Mass! It was that same piece that Leo bashed out in the dusty vestry all those years ago when he decided that I should be a singer. That first Kyrie will stay with me forever and, needless to say, I got the bass solo part, and was delighted when Andy got the tenor solo as our voices blended perfectly. I also got my first chance to work with Meredith Davies in a rollicking production of Benjamin Britten's bizarre re-working of *The Beggar's Opera* in which I played the evil gaoler, Lockit.

During the summer, I was re-engaged by the Philharmonia Chorus as they were planning a return trip to the fabulous Roman Theatre in Orange. The chorus was all men this time mostly made up of first study opera students from the London colleges so that the sound was incredible. The cast was world-class too…Barbara Hendricks as Gilda, Renato Bruson as Rigoletto and the fabulous Spanish tenor Alfredo Kraus as the Duke. I found a clip from the actual performance on YouTube (Orange 1980) and his La Donna e Mobile is as good, if not better, than I remember it, with a ridiculously long high note at the end in which he stood up from his chair to almost double the sound. The last act only has a bit of offstage chorus so we were able to slip into the square and get to the bar before the theatre emptied thousands of people looking for a drink. One very enterprising patroness bribed us with trays of 'Formidables' (very large beers) if we sang exclusively outside her bar. It worked. The audience flooded out and headed straight for the sound of a very professional male voice choir singing English and Welsh folk songs. Her bar was teeming and other bar owners looked on with no small amount of respect and chagrin.

During one performance Bruson, slightly overacting, threw himself and his considerable bulk at the courtiers to protect his daughter. *Cortigianni, vil razza danata*! I shouldered his charge and I thought he had dislocated my arm! He could have played rugby for France. We were joined by the ladies of the choir for a concert of Mozart's Requiem and Mahler's 2nd Symphony conducted by the very impressive American, Michael Tilson Thomas. It was my last trip to Orange but I loved every minute of it.

On my return to London for my second year, yet another of those bizarre coincidences happened. In the opera class, we were all invited to present an opera scene for public performance and I elected to perform the huge soliloquy *Pari siamo* and duet from Act I of Rigoletto. This was firstly, because it was fresh in my mind and secondly, because there was a very good soprano who I had in the frame that I had a bit of a crush on and she would suit the role of Gilda very well. One dreary autumnal evening, in my flat in Earl's Court Square, the telephone rang. The voice asked for me by name and said that he was from Hatfield Opera. I thought *Oh God, not another amateur opera company trying to recruit singers!* But it was much worse than that.

"How well do you know the role of Rigoletto?"

I said that much of it I knew very well and asked why.

"Well, our Rigoletto has over-sung and as a result is unable to sing tomorrow and we have a sell-out theatre."

"Tomorrow? Good grief, don't you have an understudy?"

"Afraid not and it's far too demanding for any of our amateur singers. We can pay you £200 for a single performance."

"But how could I possibly get through a performance without even an inkling of the production or stage direction, not to mention the hugeness of the actual singing role itself?"

"Yes, we've thought of that. You can use music and sing from the orchestra pit next to the conductor and the producer will dress and act the role on stage, miming the part. Please say you'll do it; the future of the company depends on it."

"How on earth did you get in touch with me?" I said, desperately playing for time.

"Ah! Well as luck would have it, the bass playing the assassin Sparafucile is a Trinity student and he said you would be the man for the job as you were working on the part anyway. I'll collect you from the station and we can have a quick rehearsal with the orchestra and conductor."

And so it was that I found myself boarding a train for Hatfield, with my score of Rigoletto and thoughts of how to murder Bloomfield, the bass who had landed me in this terrifying predicament. I arrived at the station and was duly greeted

69

by a very frazzled character who looked as if he hadn't had much sleep of late. The sight of my diminutive frame clearly didn't inspire him with confidence.

"Oh! You're a lot smaller than our last Rigoletto!"

"Well, I haven't got a hump but at least I have my voice intact," I replied, irritated.

I arrived at the theatre and found the whole orchestra waiting for me with the cast on stage including Bloomfield grinning.

"Right!" said the conductor. "We haven't much time so let's do the tricky bits. Shall we start with your big soliloquy in Act I before the duet?"

The orchestra played a chord and I proceeded…

"Pari siamo, io la lingua…" The conductor tapped his stick and the orchestra stopped.

"We are doing the opera in English, Mr Dalby."

"WHAT!!" I did my best impression of John McEnroe. "You can NOT be serious!"

The performance came after an eternity of yellow highlight marker on the small italic English translation and to be honest, I did often lapse into Italian during the fast passages but no one seemed to mind. I reached the tragic conclusion of the opera, and the curse and Gilda's dead body in the sack, to be greeted by a standing ovation from the packed house. I needed a big drink!

Chapter 11
A Change of Direction

The following term a student choir that I sometimes sang with faced a bit of a crisis. The student conductor was not a singer himself and had rather a low opinion of the musicianship of singers in general. As a result, during one rehearsal, no tenors had turned up at all and, in a huff, he resigned and stormed out of the room. Everyone who had turned up remained seated in stunned silence until one of the girls let out a suppressed guffaw which then exploded into a general mêlée of hilarity. One of the girls took charge and it was decided upon that we should have a vote on who to appoint as the new conductor. Someone suggested me, and there was a general consensus of agreement. I pleaded that, as I was not a keyboard player, I would not be suitable but that was overturned by the fact that many of the students who did play piano offered to take it in turns to accompany the choir if I was prepared to take over the conducting role. So, it was decided upon. Graham Dalby, the carefree singer, who always took the mickey out of conductors at College, was now one himself…with a conductor's ego to match!

I started off quite gently with a programme of choral music with organ. The response from the choir was immediate and not only did more singers from Trinity join but tenors and basses from other colleges too. Most of the recruiting was done in the pub and there, one evening, I chatted to a young violinist called Freddie, who had an early music group who performed Renaissance and Baroque repertoire in an authentic style. In the time it took to buy another round, we had combined our forces for a performance of Vivaldi's Gloria and Pergolesi's Magnificat. Freddie led the orchestra and I conducted both choir and orchestra for the first time. I remember we even had a viol da gamba player, who made so much noise deep breathing when he played that he almost drowned the mezzo-soprano out in the 'Domine Deus' solo.

71

That concert did it for me. I was completely hooked. Conducting really was better than anything I had experienced. I approached the College and requested to change my second study from violin to conducting. My poor fiddle teacher hid her grief as best she could. "I'm afraid I have to give up my violin lessons as I wish to do conducting as a second study." She gazed up lazily from her newspaper: "Oh, I'm so pleased! Er, for you I meant." she added quickly with an unconvincing smile and an expression of relief as when a toothache stops unexpectedly. I fully understood.

As in all things in my life, I went into this like a bull at a gate. My first conducting professor, Bernard Keefe and I clashed immediately when he said that he would not teach me unless I learnt to conduct with my right hand as he claimed, an orchestra could never read the beat in a mirror image created by a left-handed baton. Utter and complete tosh, of course, but it gave him the excuse not to have to teach me. He loathed singers and was infamous for making them look ridiculous in front of large student orchestras, keen to laugh at any jibes or jokes. I have seen young sopranos reduced to tears. My second professor was a kindly gentleman of the Old School with a slight stammer and a quivering conducting technique that defied anyone to find the downbeat. James Gaddarn was the cousin of the great Sir Malcolm Sargeant and was a choral conductor himself. He drove a vintage Bentley and the story goes that he was walking down Marylebone High Street one day, on a bright November morning, carrying his silver-topped cane. Unfortunately, in the bright Autumnal sunlight, he failed to notice a BT worker down a hole, surrounded by a fragile wooden structure to warn pedestrians. Colliding with the barrier, his cane went clattering down the hole before being stopped by the hard hat of the BT worker. Some choice expletives ensued before the angry engineer emerged from his 'ole, clutching the silver-topped cane.

"Oi fairy, you've dropped yer bleeding wand!"

"F-fairy is it? Well then, d-d-disappear!" He waved the cane at the worker, in the same manner as when exhorting the 'cellos to play up a little, before sauntering off to his next class.

Some 30 years later, I was working at the London Guildhall, for an event to mark the 200th Anniversary of Frederick Chopin. A man came up to the stage where I was performing and said there was an elderly gentleman who wished to speak with me. Fascinated, I left the orchestra, who were playing a Polonaise perfectly well without my help and went over to the table. There was the unmistakable profile of James Gaddarn, now so bent double he could barely lookup.

"Ah, Graham d…Dalby! I knew it. I'd recognise that voice anywhere!" He said. After handshakes, I returned to the stage and shortly after I noticed him leaving the proceedings. I announced to the applause of the audience that a much-loved music conductor and professor was leaving and he raised his cane above his bowed frame in acknowledgement. He left us all a few months later aged 87.

Choral conducting was all very well for me but once having got a taste of directing an orchestra, I just wanted to move on to bigger things. There was this huge church called St James Sussex Gardens, which I knew, as I had sung Jesus in the St Matthew Passion there. They were very accommodating when I asked about putting on a concert but I think they had no idea of the musical forces I was intending to bring. It was my very first experience of conducting a symphony orchestra and I chose my beloved Elgar. The 'Cockaigne Overture' is extremely tricky and definitely not for a beginner! It's a symphonic poem devoted to London Town and is scored for a vast ensemble with a military band and an organ thrown in. No four bars are the same tempo and it varies in dynamic from wistful to deafening. I still have the recording of the performance and I never cease to be amazed at the skill of those young student players in such a demanding piece. As if this wasn't loud enough, we followed with Hubert Parry's *I Was Glad*, scored for orchestra, organ and eight trumpets with the choir shouting "Vivat Regina Elizabetha!" at the top of their lungs. The second half comprised *The Nelson Mass* by Haydn; yes, the same piece Leo had got me to sing all those years ago at school in that life-changing moment in the school chapel vestry. The bass soloist was the magnificent John Noble and the tenor Nick Robertson, who had won a choral scholarship to St John's Cambridge from Dover College. After the performance, the adrenalin was pumping and many of us repaired to a nearby pub. The regulars there thanked us for the concert which they said could be heard quite clearly from the saloon bar.

The following term, I was rehearsing with James Gaddarn and the whole of the Trinity choir and orchestra, at Brompton Oratory for the Verdi Requiem. Many of us stayed after to enjoy a pint in a little pub around the back where I was introduced to the bass, Brian Kay. Being a tremendous fan of The King's Singers, I was very sad to hear he had just sung his last concert, and was now officially unemployed, as he decided where his career should go after nearly two decades with this world-renown vocal group. With tremendous impertinence, I asked him if he would like to sing the bass solo in Haydn's Creation which I was conducting the following term. He asked how many were in the orchestra and I replied only about 50, which I considered to be a small and somewhat modest group, after the monster, symphonic, ear-bleeding ensemble I had assembled at Sussex Gardens. He explained that having spent 19 years whispering close-mic'd bass booms and doo's and aah's, his voice wasn't up to singing unaided in front of a fifty-piece chamber orchestra. However, he was clearly tempted by the prospect and another pint sealed the deal. It was his first job after the King Singers and I was careful to keep the orchestra suppressed in order for his rich, sonorous bass tones to fill the lovely church of St John's Wood, which they certainly did.

Chapter 12
Upset and Tragedy

In my third and final graduate term, I was cast in the hugely amusing role of the Judge in *Trial by Jury* which we performed at a theatre just off Tottenham Court Road. I enjoyed the part enormously and was quite unprepared for the huge academic shock that awaited me. Only performing course students went on to do a fourth year and I was very much looking forward to that. Nothing could have prepared me for the shock, therefore, of receiving the incredible news that I had failed the final exam spectacularly badly. I just couldn't understand it. I had been standing in front of choirs and orchestras conducting, I had immersed myself in music history, music theory and music performance. Whilst many of my colleagues regarded music as an academic course unlikely to be followed up in their future, I had a mind only for a music career. To receive just 27% overall for both performance and academic studies seemed incredible. I had never failed to get into the finals of every song competition in French, German and English and had been awarded prizes for ensemble singing and choral conducting as well as representing the college in all opera and oratorio events. How could this be? I took my grievance and disbelief to the Academic Registrar, my old friend, Cyril Cork! He peered at me over half-moon spectacles with that disapproving look I had seen in the audition and embarked on a tirade against my conducting activities, that I had been using the college students to mount huge outside concerts that had nothing to do with Trinity but merely to fuel my bumped-up ego and continue my relentless march of self-promotion but that the exam had proved that academically I was not fit to be a Trinity student etc. He rather extended himself on the subject. When he finally ran out of steam, I thought I should try and pick out a few points. Firstly, the essay. We were asked to write on any opera by Verdi or compare the orchestrations of Berlioz and Wagner. I, of course, chose to write at very great length, on the opera Rigoletto. By chance,

Lady Scholey had given me a definitive book on the opera by the iconic baritone, Tito Gobbi. There wasn't much I didn't know about the opera; it was based on Le Roi s'Amuse by Victor Hugo and got itself on the banned list in France rather like Beaumarchais' Le Marriage de Figaro had for Mozart's Le Nozze di Figaro. Verdi also ran foul of the Venetian authorities who were in the pocket of the Austrian Hapsburg Empire. The king, Francis I of France, had to be changed to an Italian Duke of Mantua and loads of other political details changed in the libretto before it could be performed at La Fenice in Venice in 1851. The original title 'La Maledizione' was changed to 'Rigoletto' and the first-night sell-out was a triumph, with delivery boys whistling 'La Donne e Mobile' in the streets ever after. All of this and much more I had written without pause over the three-hour allotted time. I asked the glowering figure behind the desk *who* had marked my paper with such a low score, as I should love to have coffee or dinner with him/her in order to ascertain what I had actually omitted on the subject, as it was of great interest to me. At this, the Registrar became highly indignant and said that he would be writing to my grant authority and that I would not be returning to Trinity for a fourth year. I left the office with a calm but steely "I'll be back" look at the Registrar, who now had the contented countenance of a Jersey cow who has just passed wind after a stomach pain.

This, of course, was war! But what to do? I felt powerless but a rankling sense of injustice drove me. I took a bus journey to Enfield, having made an appointment to see my Grant Authority. I was well prepared and took all the programmes of every Trinity concert in which I had featured as a soloist, the prizes I had been awarded, the song competitions and the flyers for the external concerts I had organised and conducted. I told them the 'Rigoletto story' about the marking and was met with unexpected sympathy and support. They were used to students getting sent down for shirking and doing no work but I was clearly not of that type. They had invested a considerable sum in my education so far and didn't want it wasted if they could help it and help it they did. They wrote to the college requesting an independent assessment of my written papers, the history and the harmony but were refused by the College. Then the Principal got to hear of it as the wonderful John Wakefield (head of opera) had lobbied him on my behalf. A compromise was immediately suggested by Meredith (Principal) with the wisdom of Solomon. Given my indefatigable and assiduous contribution to the musical life at Trinity, he said it was only reasonable to offer this student an opportunity to re-take the exam in its entirety in the Hilary Term and with outside adjudication as well as internal. Reprieve!

I spent a peaceful Christmas at the family home in Hartley Witney and have a photo of myself and my brother John, beer in hand, singing a rowdy a cappella duet of *Christmas is Coming the Geese are Getting Fat*. All seemed well.

I returned in the deep Winter of 1984, determined not only to pass with a clear margin but with the equivalent of an Honours at over 80%. I didn't even audition for the big college concert at the Fairfield Hall in Croydon, which was *Delius' Mass of Life* conducted by Meredith Davies, even though I loved Delius as a composer. I sang in the choir as a rank-and-file bass.

It was March 26th, Mutti's birthday and Mother's Day had just passed on Sunday. A dutiful son and perhaps a bit of a 'mummy's boy', I had arranged for the local florist to deliver a big bouquet of flowers for her joint Mother's Day/Birthday wishes. I had travelled down to Croydon by train for the rehearsal of the *Delius Mass of Life* and afterwards, I and a gang of singers went out in search of a cheap eatery in this gloomy suburb town. When we returned to the concert hall the others went off to change but I, seeing a phone box in the foyer, said I needed to make a call to wish my mother a happy birthday. My father answered the phone with a sepulchral voice and in answer to my question replied with all the tact of someone who has just failed his Samaritans audition:

"Haven't you heard? We've been trying to reach you all day. John's dead!"

I suppose there is no easy way of breaking news like that. The high-ceilinged foyer reeled and my ears created a high-pitched hum. I couldn't take it in, nor summon up the thousands of questions that immediately sprang to mind. I guessed a motorbike accident or something similar. Nothing could have prepared me for the horror story that unfurled. It appeared, that on a rainy Sunday night, the 25th, John had gone out on his motorbike and stopped at a pub and had had a pint of lager. He then travelled to the Fleet railway line, scaled the high fence with a pillow (for comfort no doubt) and had settled down on the railway track with a Walkman, awaiting the London-bound train. Nothing was seen or noticed until blood was spotted on the front carriage at Waterloo. My flowers had arrived, just as a policewoman was explaining these appalling events to my distraught mother, who thought they might be from John with a note giving some form of explanation for this extraordinary "lapse of reason", as the coroner put it. I replaced the telephone and leant against a wall to support my legs that seemed ready to give way from under me. I stared into nothingness as I tried to grapple with the enormity and horror of what I was trying to take in when a voice from the tannoy brought me round.

"Ladies and Gentlemen, please make your way into the auditorium as the concert will begin shortly." I made my way like a sleepwalker, to the artists changing room and was greeted by a fraught Andy, looking immaculate in evening dress.

"Come on! We're on in five minutes." Then he stopped, knowing instinctively that something was very wrong. I began to get changed helped by a few friends and mumbled that my brother had been killed. I went on and don't remember much about it but trying desperately to concentrate on the music and blank my mind to the appalling images that kept invading it.

At the interval, I shuffled off with the others and was greeted by the orchestral manager, Jeff Josephs, who thrust a large brandy into my hand. Trinity had been contacted and had got the message across to the concert hall in Croydon. He stated that, of course, I didn't need to go on for the second half. The brandy however had cleared my senses and I knew that I just had to keep going, so I went on, comforted by fellow singers to my left and to my right. I held it all together throughout and only broke down whilst waiting for the train back to London, realising it was the same track that ran down to Fleet.

The next few weeks were very difficult. The funeral was in a disused Jacobean churchyard which the vicar agreed to as a compromise, given the ludicrous ruling that you can't be buried in consecrated ground if you have taken your own life. The empty stone church was far more beautiful than the ugly Victorian red-brick monstrosity down by the Hartley Witney village green and was situated on a hilltop over-looking rolling Hampshire countryside. It was April and the churchyard and surrounding area was a mass of yellow daffodils under a blue sky. The cricket season was upon us but John, white-flannelled, would never again elegantly dispatch the red ball to the boundary with a timely roll of the wrists. We sang Purcell's *Thou Knowest Lord the Secret of our Hearts* in the Victorian church before walking up the hill to lay John Cameron Barrington Dalby (30/01/62–25/03/84) to rest in the bright, Spring sunshine in his beloved Hampshire. He never left a note explaining why he chose to leave us. He was just twenty-two.

With all this on my mind, I had the re-take of my Licentiate diploma to attend to. I stayed in every evening, practising various chord sequences and Bach harmonisations and, as it was a Delius anniversary, I read up on that composer in particular, memorising some important music quotations. When the day of the paper arrived I turned it over to discover the Bach chorale (they give you the first two bars and you finish it in the style of) was one I was sure I had sung before and quickly laid down the bass line before accurately adding the other harmony parts. The other questions I finished in good time, giving me ample time to extend myself in the history essay part. And there it was! 'Choose to write about the life and works of either Edward Elgar or Frederick Delius'. Within seconds, I was immersed in Fred's early life in the orange plantations of Florida where his first composition *The Florida Suite* was written. It was given its premiere in a beer cellar in Leipzig by a student orchestra, mostly friends of Delius', in return for the contents of a barrel of beer! As the dying, blind Delius' life with his amanuensis, Eric Fenby ('are the swallows late this year?') played out of my fountain pen, I thought that this was almost as good as my Rigoletto essay. I left the examination centre in the knowledge that, with a fair adjudicator, I must have reached the 60% pass required.

Just the practical part now. I had planned a completely new programme for this recital which demanded an opera aria, an oratorio solo, an Arie antiche, an unaccompanied folksong and an art song in French or German. I chose *Eugene Onegin's aria* by Tchaikovsky, in Russian, *Verdi's Requiem Confutatis*, in Latin, *Pieta Signore*, in Italian, *The Trees they Grow so High* in English and *The Erlkönig* by Schubert, in German. My accompanist was a fellow, cricket-playing, beer- drinking, funny and wonderful friend called Paul Chilvers, who is still there as senior répétiteur and played for my daughter Cassie's graduate recital at Trinity in 2018!

We achieved practically full marks but for a slight lapse in intonation in the folk song in which Paul didn't play. Then the written results were released. I had achieved a combined score of 87%. It was the highest score of all the students with the exception of a brilliant 'cellist called Franny who got 89% and was generally regarded as a genius, with perfect pitch, and who led the 'cello section in my orchestral concerts. Today, she is a head of department at a very expensive school in Clapham and is still, I believe, a genius. But I do still wonder how it was possible to fail so badly and pass with honours within a term. Could it have been some dodgy work at the crossroads? I'll ask the lawyers if I can leave that in.

The Songs of The Fleet
For Baritone and
Orchestra
C.V. Stanford

Snape 1984

**EASTERTIME
AT THE MALTINGS**

**SUFFOLK SCHOOLS
JUBILEE CHOIR**

Chorus Master - David Ingate

SUFFOLK SCHOOLS' ORCHESTRA

Leader - Judith Linn

with

GRAHAM DALBY - Baritone

Conductor: KEITH SHAW

Te Deum in C	- Haydn
Easter Festival Overture	- Rimsky Korsakov
Intermezzo and Easter Hymn	- Mascagni
Matinees Musicales	- Britten
Songs of the Fleet	- Stanford

SNAPE MALTINGS
Wednesday 18th April 1984 - 7.30 p.m.

My relief and joy, combined with the grief I was wrestling with, was lightened by Meredith Davies asking me if I thought I was up to singing a big solo at 'The Maltings', Snape, the Mecca of English music, designed and commissioned by Benjamin Britten. It was a huge programme, with a huge orchestra and choir, made up of the Suffolk schools and featuring *The Songs of the Fleet* for baritone, choir and orchestra by Charles Villiers Stanford. It was just a few weeks after burying my brother, but I had to do it. Meredith also added his commiserations on my news and congratulations at my recent exam success with a comment upon the incongruity of the two results, with much chin rubbing.

To sing at the Maltings, Snape was a dream come true and the acoustics were unbelievable. Despite the orchestra of about 90 and the choir of about 60, I could hear my solo voice pinging back from the far walls and I didn't have to fight to be heard at all. What a concert hall! I should just like to end this chapter of tragedy with a final tragedy that had happened on the same day as my brother's untimely demise...

My mother had, understandably, taken John's death very hard; her youngest, and with no explanation. My father was away in Africa trying to swing some deal or other and she was left alone with her thoughts. These turned to the dark side and incredibly, she managed to set up some kind of homemade Ouija board in which she managed, quite alone, to generate enough electricity to move the glass around at speed with her finger still attached to it. Some of the words spelt out are too ghastly to repeat here but she at length managed to contact someone who seemed friendly and sympathetic. In answers to the various questions of "who are you?" and "where is John?" she only got "George, Graham's friend", "he's not here, he's not here", "he's OK but he's not here".

The following day, Mutti phoned me in London at my flat.

"Have you got a friend called George?" I answered that I had, an Irish tenor who had left the college but with whom I had shared a flat. She asked if he was OK and I replied, to the best of my knowledge, that he was fine. I was concerned for her so I agreed to call George and call her back. George answered, in his lilting Belfast accent, to give me the good news that he had secured a place in the chorus at Covent Garden Opera. All good. I replaced the receiver and immediately it rang again. It was John Touhey, the BBC World Service presenter. I began to apologise for not being in touch and told him my dreadful news which, being a trained Samaritan, he listened to with great sympathy and sensitivity for a full 15 minutes before telling me why he had called. His close friend, the airline pilot George Bressey, had been driving back from Gatwick to their cottage near Wells in Somerset, around 11:00 at night on 25th March, when he misjudged a sharp turning on a tiny country lane and the car careered off into a ditch. George was pronounced dead at the scene with no one else being involved. George was a meticulous driver and John Touhey has always suspected suicide. But it was at more or less the same time on the same evening that my brother John had taken his life.

"More things in Heaven and Earth, [Horatio] than are dreamt of in your philosophy." (Hamlet)

Chapter 13
New Friends

My final term at Trinity was a very pleasant one indeed. We worked hard on a wonderful operetta by Offenbach, called 'La Vie Parisienne', to be performed at The Bloomsbury Theatre and conducted by the famous Sadlers Wells conductor Alexander 'Sandy' Farris, the composer of the television music to *Upstairs Downstairs*. We had a cast of very fine soloists and a strong chorus made up of next year's soloists to be. I was delighted with my role as a naughty old Swedish aristocrat, Baron Gondremark, which I hammed up, with the help of a monocle, which I used to pop out of my eye as an expression of astonishment and which never failed to get a laugh. The young Irish producer was full of ideas and the performance was a riot of melodies, fabulous costumes, courtesy of ENO, and much hi-jinks and hilarity on stage during the week's performance. I have listened to it recently on YouTube and though the recording is basic, the quality of the playing from the orchestra is evident and apart from my dreadful attempt at a Swedish accent, the whole show is a delight on the ear and eye. My ego was boosted by a very favourable review from Opera Magazine who loved the production and added something along the lines of "Graham Dalby's secure baritone would grace any professional stage"…coo!

Perhaps because of that favourable review, I received a letter from a body calling itself 'The European Opera Centre', asking me if I would audition for them. We met at a studio in Wigmore Street, and they asked me to sing two pieces by Verdi: Rigoletto and Il Trovatore. It was then explained to me that this was, in fact, a Summer school in Belgium for advanced opera students from around the world, where the coaches would include Nicolai Gedda, the great Swedish tenor, and senior members of the Guildhall Opera faculty. They then explained that the central work to be performed was Puccini's 'Gianni Schicchi', in a costumed production, and concert highlights from Pagliacci, Il Trovatore and Rigoletto. When I explained that my funds had pretty much dried up, they quickly added that it would be a scholarship, with everything found except my travel, as it was late notice and the singer from Russia had failed in his visa attempt. This was marvellous but it did have one big drawback which I shall endeavour to explain…

It was the beginning of the new academic year, my last at Trinity, and the Freshers seemed absurdly young to me, some not even yet 18. I was already 23 when I joined the College so was now 27. It must have been late September when the Students Union organised the usual Freshers Ball at a venue that was part of the University of London, just off the Tottenham Court Road. I arrived very late as I had been singing opera arias in my lovely restaurant in Chancery Lane, for the grand fee of £25 plus a bottle of wine and a bowl of pasta! It was called 'Spaghetti Opera' and I sang there three times a week to an audience, mostly drawn from the legal profession, which made me easily the richest student at Trinity. Arriving by taxi and dressed as for my recent performance, in evening attire, I was appalled to see practically none of the freshers had made any effort to dress for the occasion and many of them were now in an advanced state of intoxication. After about 20 minutes of observing this Bacchanalian Rout, I decided that this was best left to the younger set, especially as some young ex-airline stewardess, now a wannabe soprano, had just drunkenly offered me my heart's desire if I gave her the solo part in an upcoming Mozart piece I was conducting! I hailed a taxi and, just as we were pulling out into Tottenham Court Road, a young woman fell in front of us, seriously endangering the bodywork of the black cab. The driver stopped abruptly with a colourful Bow Bells oath. I said I thought she was one of ours and on questioning the young lady, it turned out to be so, and very inebriated she was too. She appeared to be alone and not badly hurt, so I told her to get in and we could get her home. When she told me she lived in Hampstead, I realised that this would clear me out as I would have to get the cab there and back, being about a one hour round journey. I suggested we head back to my place to take a look at the minor injuries she had sustained. My flat was just behind Selfridges, so after a short journey, we alighted at St James' Place, Marylebone. I got her up the stairs, cleaned up the abrasions and popped her into bed, where she at once fell into a dreamless coma. I closed the door and went to make up the fold-out bed. In the morning, I went in with a cup of tea and put on some music. She aroused painfully, asking the usual questions of "where am I? Who are you? How did I get here? Did we…?"

I answered them all in order, and on answering the last, she asked petulantly, "Why? Am I so unattractive?" I told her that she was very slightly worse for wear and that there were rules about that sort of thing. I have heard the same scene played out in *High Society* between Grace Kelly and Frank Sinatra, almost word for word but at that time, neither of us had seen that film. As it dawned upon her that I had, in fact, been her knight in a shining black cab, she began cooing her appreciation and I was astonished when she asked me to use the phone to order a taxi to take her home.

"Have you got enough money?" I asked, hoping she wasn't going to ask me to lend her the fare, which would have been all of last night's earnings and some.

"Oh no," she replied, "I just put it on Daddy's account. He wouldn't want me using public transport." *Who was this girl?* I thought. She had told me her name which I had forgotten but remembered it was the same as a famous Italian opera singer. She left with a sunny disposition that belied the condition I had found her in the previous night. I remembered her name then, Fiorenza, as in Fiorenza Cosotto, the famous opera soprano.

In November that term, I was conducting a very large concert of Elgar and Parry when this same young lady came up to me at the end to introduce her tall and distinguished-looking parents. They thanked me for looking after their daughter, and invited me to lunch with them on Sunday, at their home in Hampstead. I duly attended and arrived at their home, just behind Kenwood House. The hallway boasted a magnificent harpsichord with a stunning Italian Renaissance painting on the underside of the open lid, a gravity-defying sculpture 'Dolphin and boy' by David Wynn, and three of the maddest spaniels who skidded about on the Italianate tiled floor. The lady of the house had a beauty and regal bearing not dissimilar to Princess Alexandra, with that same ability to make you feel as if you are a very special guest and that she must find out all about you. The host, a portly and amiable city banker of very high standing, extended a warm greeting and pushed a glass of ice-cold champagne into my hand. He had a charming smile and a twinkle in his eye as of a man who has drunk deep from the cup of life.

I have been diverted from my European Opera Centre story but this now ties up. Young Fiorenza and I became inseparable friends at Trinity but she was concerned that I didn't have a girlfriend and decided I would be perfect for a friend of hers whose mother, a Canadian, was very good friends with Fiorenza's mother Lady S. It was like an arranged marriage but when she did arrive, I was pleasantly surprised and she likewise. Joanna was a classic English rose, despite being half Canadian. She was studying Art at the Courtauld Institute just around the corner from Trinity but lived in a stunning house in Parsons Green with her mother, an interior decorator, who at that time was away in Canada. If I had any doubts about Joanna, which I didn't, they were dispelled when she invited me around for dinner and cooked the most delicious meal I had ever eaten. I know woodpigeon was involved, for it transpired that she had completed a cookery course with the great Pru Leith and was practically a professional chef. The way to a man's heart! Joanna or Joey as everyone called her was also the goddaughter of Sir David, Fiorenza's father. The official approval from Hampstead came when both Joey and I were invited to spend the summer at a stunning villa in Fiesole, on the hill overlooking the olive trees and down to the Arno, the Ponte Vecchio and the red-tiled magnificence of the Duomo di Firenze built with Medici money of the great Florentine bankers.

Joey excitedly phoned her mother in Canada. "Mummy! I've got a boyfriend!"

"That's great news darling, what's his name?" Phone-line crackles…

"It's Graham."

[In Canadian accent]…"GRIM!! What kinda name is that??"

Joey falls about laughing and never corrects Patsy, her mother, who has a wicked sense of humour and, I'm sure, heard perfectly well.

So, Grim, I became and am still called that by my friends, although the many Italians in Fiorenza's circle found 'Grimmy' much easier and more Italianate.

Now the tough bit. The European Opera Centre was a great opportunity but it clashed with the invite to go and bathe deeply in rich Florentine culture for two weeks with my new girlfriend, eating fabulous food and basking in the warm Tuscan sunshine. What to do? I went to see Lady S to tell her of my travails.

Her eyes widened.

"But darling, of course, you must go, it's about your future but you can still spend five days with us and I'll arrange to get you from Florence to Strasbourg by train and from there to Alden Biesen. So, it's all settled then, you're coming with us!"

The admiration in which I held this lady could not be expressed in words.

Graduation Day was hot and I enjoyed flouncing around Wigmore Street in my academic gown, hood and mortarboard, having just been presented with my LTCL diploma by the eminent conductor Sir Charles Groves, in the Wigmore

Hall. My parents attended and I suggested we take tea at Claridge's, so I billowed down in my gown, across Oxford Street to Brooke Street, home of the great English hotel. We were greeted by a liveried waiter and shown into the high-ceilinged drawing room where tea was being served, to the strains of a piano trio, who were playing hits of Ivor Novello, Vivien Ellis and Noël Coward, at a reverential dynamic. It appeared to be almost entirely populated by Americans, who were vociferous in their congratulations of this newly crowned academic. Mutti beamed proudly, and I watched with amusement, a young and loud American being told in no uncertain terms, that he could not remain in the room unless he put on his jacket and agreed to wear the tie the footman was holding. It was quite a smart silk tie and the American capitulated under the unrelenting eye of English pomposity or as he so quaintly put it, "English Bullshit!" Oh, to be English! My father enjoyed the afternoon slightly less and narrowly became the victim of a cardiac arrest, when the aforementioned liveried footman, presented him with the bill. I think I only averted the cardiac failure when I suggested I buy him a large pink gin in a lovely little pub I knew nearby called the Golden Eagle in Marylebone Lane. This pub, though tiny and Victorian, boasted an upright piano and an elderly lady called Annie, who used to stand in for Carroll Gibbons with his orchestra, 'The Savoy Orpheans', in the 30s. As a result, she knew by heart practically every song from the 20s, 30s and 40s, and always encouraged me to sing along. My parents left and I moved on to the Angel Tavern in Marylebone High Street to join my revelling colleagues, still sporting mortarboards, with flowing ale and wine, like a scene out of the *Student Prince* in Heidelberg. Life was good in the knowledge that I still had a fabulous trip to Florence and a two week stay in a Belgium château to look forward to. After that though, heaven only knew.

Chapter 14
Florence and Alden Biesen

Joey and I took a flight to Pisa and then a sweltering train to Firenze, which rattled and rocked all the way, in a journey that seemed endless. We took a taxi to Fiesole, with blissful air-conditioning, up the steep, dusty slope, through the olive groves and were dropped outside two imposing steel gates. Upon pressing the bell, it appeared I had unleashed a Baskervillian hound with slavering jaws and a thunderous deep-throated baritone bark, interspersed with a rumbling growl, that could be measured on the Richter Scale. Joey and I instinctively backed away from the slowly opening gates. A voice from inside shouted, "Iago, vieni qui! Vieni qui!"

Iago?? I thought, *Dear God! What kind of hell-hound was behind that gate?"* But Iago didn't "vieni qui" instead he squeezed through the gap in the opening gate and bounded up to us, still clutching each other, and thinking, *we're gonna die here!*

But once I had seen Iago, I realised he was, in fact, a beautiful black and tan Doberman, probably not more than three years old and full of fun and energy. I stretched out my hand which he sniffed and licked and we became best of friends for the next five days. The gardener came puffing up behind my new canine buddy, gasping apologies.

"Scusi Signor, Scusi Signorina, prego…" and ushered us into the villa's beautiful gardens, which also sported a tennis court, a swimming pool and a breath-taking view of Florence, some four hundred feet below. Sandy (Lady S) was paddling her feet by the side of the pool in sunglasses and swimsuit like someone at a Cole Porter party and waved with apologies that she hadn't expected us so soon and that Bruno would show us to our rooms. Someone was playing the piano upstairs and I knew at once, from the ear-piercing squeal of delight as she rushed to greet us, that it was Fiorenza! Another friend was in the kitchen whom I had met at Hampstead, a lovely Greek lady called Savina and an

American cousin called Julie, along with Fiorenza's teenage brother, Christopher. We ate on the veranda, shaded from the fierce Tuscan sun, a meal of delicious Italian simplicity, of prosciutto, bruschetta, Parma hams and ciabatta bread with pesto and olives, various kinds of pasta, sweet tomatoes just picked and ice-cold white wine with nectarines. The table was a mass of colour and we all chatted gaily. I felt really close to heaven at that time. A game of tennis after lunch with Christopher confirmed my thoughts that I should have played Julie, the American cousin, with whom I later played and we were equally matched. Christopher was a muscular 16-year-old with a keen eye and a powerful serve. Tennis was his game. Not so me, I preferred the hard red ball and willow.

The five days passed so quickly I can barely remember them. Sandy was herself a gifted artist and Joey a Courtauld Institute student so it was only natural she wanted to show us the Uffizi Gallery and others, where her own children had taken little interest. I learnt more about Art in the company of those two in five days than I had learnt in a lifetime to that date. One evening, Sandy took us to a famous restaurant in Florence and treated us to truffles. I had never eaten such a delicacy before. It was an OMG moment. The waiters bowed and scraped to 'Signora Sandy' as she chatted to them gaily in perfect Italian.

Soon it was time to say goodbye. I had kept my voice in training with Fiorenza accompanying me at the piano in an aria from Faust, which was not too difficult for the piano, as she was a concert pianist and not an accompanist, big difference. Sandy took me down to the American Express office by the station to get the tickets she had ordered. The cabaret as we waited was fabulous.

[Overweight, sweating American tourist enters irately and shouts at immaculately dressed Italian].

"Hey, Buddy! What's the big idea? I said I wanted to see the Palazzo San Marco so you sent me to this place and there's no Doge's Palace!"

[Sandy and I suppressing hysterics. Even larger American lady enters hot and breathless]:

"Excuse me, sir, can you help me? I just gotta get to Florence by tomorrow."

"Signora, this eez Firenze. Firenze eeez Florence!"

"Is that a fact?? Goddamn! Then where the hell was I yesterday??"

I got my tickets and had already said my farewells to Joey and the others at the villa. Joey was suffering terribly from allergic mosquito bites that for some reason, took absolutely no interest in me. I had been immune since Singapore. So, Sandy waved me off on the next part of my Summer vacation for the long journey to Strasbourg. I changed at Strasbourg at what must be, the largest station in the world, and had a beer and sandwich in a station café that had all the air of a wartime film set. I was expecting two black leather coated men with collars turned up to walk up to me and shout "Papers!!" as I fumbled for my forged documents in my Colditz-made coat. I boarded a very inferior train and headed North into Belgium for the final furlong where an official did, indeed, enter my carriage and ask to see ticket and passport. But, on sight of my proud blue British passport, and the requirement by Her Britannic Majesty's Secretary of State to allow me to pass freely without let or hindrance, he just sniffed and handed it back to me as if there was a bad smell. And we fought two World Wars for these people! I got the impression the Belgies didn't have a very high opinion of British travellers. When I arrived at Alden Biesen, a car was waiting to take me to the Château. It was very impressive with a moat, pointed turrets and a magnificent chapel attached to it. The other singers would be arriving in the morning, I was told, so it was a bit like being at my prep school when I spent the first night alone. Well, actually, not much of the first night. Outside the Château was an inn; a proper inn just like the one you see in Asterix cartoons. It had a thatched roof and lattice windows, which emitted a yellow glow and the swirls of smoke and the smell of burning logs (for it was quite a chilly night for early August) gave it a very warm and welcoming aspect. I hurried towards it, hoping for some company, conversation and some of that famous Belgian beer. I lifted the wooden latch and pushed the heavy door open. I walked up and politely asked in French, which beer they would recommend. I asked a pink barmaid with impressive forearms: "Bon Soir Madam, je voudrais essayer une bonne bière Belge, s'ilvous plaît."

Silence…not just from the barmaid but the whole inn had now stopped to listen. I had just come from Strasbourg and no one seemed to have any difficulty understanding my imperfect French there. What could be the matter? It was a bilingual country. I then tried again in German, as we were very close to the border, although why I just didn't speak English I can't recall.

"Entschuldigung bitte, aber ich würde gerne eine gutes Belgisches Bier probieren."

Some tough eggs sat behind me, started mumbling and grumbling.

"What do you want and where do you come from?" said the beefy barmaid.

"Oh, you speak English, I'm so sorry."

She laughed, much to my relief, as it was starting to get a bit thick in that inn and I imagined, the tough eggs were debating which window to throw me out of.

"Ah! So, you must be English as Americans never say 'I'm so sorry' at the end of every sentence. Only English people say that."

"Yes, yes, quite so but my dear old thing, do you think I might get a drink; I've been travelling all day?"

"Of course, we have one hundred and sixty-five different beers here. But you must ask in Flemish."

"Ah!"

After a few minutes, to the mirth of the locals, I managed to say:

"Ik will so graak en pincher als du blieft," or something along those lines.

A huge roar of approval from the locals and a large beer arrives with the news that it is on the house. "You have been a good cabaret but please do not speak French in here and absolutely not German."

I left the inn at 02:30 with a wide grin on my face and staggered back over the drawbridge into my castle for the night, having learnt a little about local politics and a lot about the strength of Belgian beer.

The following day singers began to arrive from all the four corners of the earth. From Japan, a beautiful, petite soprano, who sang the part of Schicchi's daughter Lauretta, and stopped the show every night when it came to 'O Mio Babbino Caro'. From America and Canada three tenors; not very good, and a soprano, pretty good. From Czechoslovakia, a tenor, tall and blond, good-looking and modest (unheard of in a tenor) and a voice of such beauty that he had the ladies swooning. From Spain, a good, powerful Latino tenor voice with strong, secure top notes, which he warmed up every morning in the shower, as he went for the top C again and again, cracking each time, until he finally got it and held it for about a minute, before emerging in a towel with the single self-approval "Eeh!" From Trinidad, a good tenor who sang *Vesti la giubba* from Pagliacci in the concerts. From England, a very fine mezzo (Jady Pearl, Glyndebourne) and another good soprano, one roughish baritone and another outstanding baritone (the late Rob Poulton, Glyndebourne), also a world-class bass in Peter Rose (Metropolitan-New York).

From Germany and Holland, two very fine sopranos and a reasonable tenor. Oh yes, and me! It was an impressive and talented international line-up of fine young opera voices. We also had a large seventy-piece local orchestra who were pretty good. The whole place had a holiday atmosphere but how we worked!

Paul Hamburger was one of the coaches with Stephen Wilder, who went on to be assistant Chorus Master at Covent Garden. Gianni Schicchi was all set in Medieval Florence, so it was lovely to hear everyone singing about the city I had just left. There is no chorus and we all had solos and ensembles to learn and a lot of character-acting as the horrible, grasping relatives of Buoso Donato's family bitterly contesting his will via the clever and wily Gianni Schicchi. There was hilarity on stage once when the very substantial bass, Peter Rose, fell into a large wicker laundry-basket, intended for the body of the deceased Donato, and I couldn't get him out, he weighing in at some 17 stone and wedged firmly. We all continued singing, desperately trying to suppress our laughter and aching ribs with the whole cast trying to watch the conductor, corpsing madly and tears running down our make-up. The Flemish conductor, Ernest Maes, was furious and during the interval, we got a lecture on professionalism. Once he'd left the room, I said, "Ah, the importance of being Ernest!" Once you've gone, you've gone, darlings and the dressing room was just one hysterical mass of singers jaw-achingly lost and laughing uncontrollably until we finally managed to pull it together for the second half.

We toured Amsterdam, Aachen and several German and Dutch venues until the Grand Finale in Brussels to end the tour; a huge theatre of 2,500 seats, and a French-speaking capital and a Flemish European opera school. Never mind that the singers came from all over the world. The orchestra was Flemish, as was the conductor. 40 people turned up on an otherwise totally boycotted concert in the Belgian Euro capital in a show of shameful internal friction. What a sad ending to an otherwise sell-out tour and what a sad indictment of a people that believe politics and rivalries are more important than music and art.

Chapter 15
Out into the World (Again)

I returned to England with just my tiny income from Spaghetti Opera and began scouring around for work. A singing lutenist by the name of Martin Best needed three male and three female singers for a strange project. A concert tour of a series of songs written by Alfonso X of Spain 'El Sabio' (The wise) required a small chorus of six with his ensemble of early music specialists. The songs were all performed in Gallo-Portuguese and dated from around 1100. Well, this was different. We performed at some marvellous venues including Eton College and Salisbury Cathedral and finally recorded them in a ground-breaking new format, called Compact Disc, for a company pioneering this new digital technique, Nimbus Records.

I continued looking for work when I came upon an advert in 'The Stage' for male opera singers; they needed two tenors, two baritones and two basses. The audition was at The Royal Opera House again! The company was called Nexus Opera and was directed by contemporary music specialist, Lionel Friend. I didn't know this so I just rocked up with the same Verdi aria that I knew pretty well from Macbeth. I achieved a good final top note and the director nodded and muttered 'bravo' almost to himself. I left the opera house with a good feeling this time. Sure enough, a few days later, the letter arrived with the offer of a short contract at quite a decent rate of pay. The other singers were very good too, including my good friend and fine baritone the late Robert Poulton, with whom I had shared a room in Alden Biesen and a tenor (now well-known) called Charles Daniels. But the work was not to be a good rollicking sing by Verdi, Puccini or even Mozart. It was one of the hardest pieces I've ever had to learn. It was called 'Curlew River' by Benjamin Britten. The good news, though, was that it was to be filmed for BBC 2 in Wells Cathedral and performed live for the Bath Festival and again for the Proms in the Royal Albert Hall, being broadcast live for Radio 3. My very good friend, the BBC World Service broadcaster, John Touhey, had retired to Wells following the tragic death of his partner George, and invited me to stay in George's room in his beautiful cottage, ten minutes' walk from the cathedral. I drove down to Somerset in my little Mini with Rob, both of us singing along to an opera tape, and looking forward to a fortnight of well-paid work. George's room was just as he'd left it, with his BA uniform and pilots' hat in the wardrobe, and his things untouched. I took very great care not to disturb anything. Rehearsing in the cathedral was wonderful and John's hospitality lavish, being an excellent cook. One evening, the cast was invited to a reception by one of the Bath Festival sponsors who provided a large quantity of pink Laurent Perrier Champagne. We all drank in moderation, it seems, as there was a lot left over so, each singer who wished to, took a bottle home. Still, there was a case left so, as I was the last to leave, I felt I had to help the catering lady out who said she didn't drink and didn't want to lug it back and could I take it off her hands. This pretty pink fizz retails at around £65.00 a bottle. With great reluctance, I agreed. John and I sat up late into the night, playing music from his vast record collection, at an owl-disturbing volume, whilst enjoying several bottles of this very fine champagne by a log fire.

The film was made, the performances done, and it was time to head back to the 'Smoke' for the final concert at The Royal Albert Hall. Somebody had the great idea of us doing it all in costume and processing, through the stalls and the Promenaders, wearing our monks' habits which we had used for the film. This was a truly weird experience but the 'Prommers' were as good as gold and stood silently as we walked through them, singing the plainsong Britten had written, which changes every time it repeats in mind-boggling variants so difficult to remember. With just six singers, everyone had to be pinpoint accurate, especially as it was being broadcast live. Sadly, I have no witty anecdote, just to say that the next time I performed at the Royal Albert Hall, it was to be very different. It was a chance meeting with an extraordinary person and as these chance meetings in our lives are wont to do, it changed my life enormously. If I hadn't picked up Fiorenza from the pavement in Tottenham Court Road that night, I would never have been invited to a drinks party in a Kensington flat given by the eccentric and loveable Francis Mander and his pretty girlfriend Georgie, who had been at school with Fiorenza at West Heath School (whilst Princess Diana was Head Girl there).

The room was crowded and noisy and full of loud cocktail voices that were known then as Sloane Rangers. A stocky chap came up to me and asked me in a nervous, husky and shy way, who I knew. When I replied "Fiorenza", his face lit up and he proffered the information I already knew about his girlfriend Georgie. I realised this was the host, Francis.

He pulled over, and then said to Georgina, "Darling, darling come and meet this chap, he knows Fiorenza."

"Oh, yes? She was the best pianist in our school and went to a music college somewhere."

"Yes, she goes to Trinity where I was, that's how we met."

"Oh, you're a musician too, golly how clever you all are! Aren't they, Franky?"

"Yes, that's really good, really good. I'm organising a ball on VE Day in a couple of weeks to celebrate 40 years of peace in Europe and we've booked the Angus Gibson Discotheque for dancing. Wouldn't it be really great, really great if you could do some music or something? What d'you think, what d'you think?"

"Well, I…I…well, it's not the sort of thing I do. You see, I'm a conductor and an opera singer and I think what you really need is a swing band or something like that."

His face fell with disappointment but lit up again in recognition as Joey had appeared at my elbow.

"Hello Francis, great party! I see you've met Grimmy."

I realised that we hadn't even exchanged names and here he was offering me a job.

"Yes, darling, I was just explaining to Francis that Swing music is not what I do."

She laughed. "What nonsense, of course you can, with all those wonderful musicians you know; it would be a piece of cake. How much does it pay?"

I looked at Joey in shock and admiration.

"Errr, I don't know…what d'you think, what d'you think?"

I did a quick mental calculation and added the cost of buying the music, not having a clue where I might get it, and paying the boys and a stress fee for me.

"Yes, OK, it's a deal…that's really great, really great. It's at the Hammersmith Palais and I'd like you to play as guests arrive for about an hour. That would be really great, really great."

He meandered off to greet some other guests. Joey burst out laughing.

"I should be your manager! What do you think by nearly turning him down when you haven't got any work on? You can't live on canapés and cocktails, you know."

She was right. I desperately needed the work but I didn't have much of a clue about Swing music although I had a lot of English dance band records of which I was very fond and knowledgeable.

The next day I went into Trinity to put word out that I needed jazz and swing specialists for a one-off paid gig. A trumpet player who had played in my orchestra came up to me and said, "The bloke you want is Mike Lovatt; he plays in the Trinity Swing Band and he's the best in the college at that sort of thing."

"Really? The bloke with the crooked lip and the broken teeth?" I asked incredulously.

"Oh, yes, you wanna hear him play."

"OK, if you see him can you ask him to get in touch? Thanks."

That evening I met up with Mike Lovatt for the first time in the Angel Tavern and over a beer, I knew he was just the person I was looking for. I hadn't even heard him play but I just knew. I needed his knowledge and expertise as I was way off-piste and would be on a steep learning curve. I asked him what had happened to his lip and he told me the most amazing story. He had been cycling downhill, some years before when he had come off in a terrible crash and had smashed his face into the road. Several of his front teeth were broken and his mouth was badly cut. He stayed in hospital for a while as they tried to repair the damage but when he asked the doctor if he would ever play the trumpet again, the doctor shook his head saying, "I'm afraid I think that would be out of the question given the damage to your lip." Mike told me that, after his lip had healed, he tried for six months every day to get a sound out of his trumpet or even just to create an embouchure capable of making a sound. Gradually, slowly, he worked out a way to purse his lips to create a noise through the mouthpiece and after nearly a year, he could manage to play long notes. If you have not heard of this remarkable musician, he is regarded today as one of the finest trumpet players in the land.

Chapter 16
Out of My Comfort Zone

The first real problem for those wishing to start up a Swing Band is where to get the arrangements and I didn't have a clue. Fortunately, there was a small shop near Soho called Studio Music that had a pile of dance band arrangements, mostly done by a chap called Jimmy Lally, who had a format where the band could be anything from three-piece to an eighteen-piece and it would still work. The trouble was that most of these arrangements sounded far too modern and not at all like the sound of the wonderful bands I had on my records. Notwithstanding, I purchased a bundle of these charts and organised the first rehearsal. Some of these charts we still have like *In the Mood*, which sounds perfectly well. The small ensemble of one trumpet, one trombone, two saxes, piano, bass and drums settled easily into these arrangements and where there was a vocal, I added one. After two hours, we had a set together and were ready for the Hammersmith Palais. We all met up at Trinity on VE Day and piled into two taxis and set off for Hammersmith with instruments and drums sticking out everywhere. An empty cab pulled up alongside us at the lights and clearly knew our driver.

"Ere Bob! 'Oo've you got in the back there mate, 'Arry Gold and 'is Pieces of Eight?"

[Ah, hilarious!]

We arrived and set up our wire music stands and the keyboard in the huge ballroom that was known as the Palais de Danse. Soon, droves of smartly attired youngsters began pouring in, some in wartime outfits, others in bright meringue-sized ballgowns, so popular in the 80s, and all speaking loudly in the Sloane Wah-Wah dialect that usually begins: "Well ekchully, ay reeely don't think Melissa's going to make it as she got plaarstered at the 'One Far One' last night"…[shrieks with laughter]. The 151 Club was a favourite Sloane hang-out, in the King's Road, which stayed open till 2:30am weeknights.

We struck up and everybody noticed us (for about thirty seconds) and then returned to the stories they were telling each other as the champagne flowed. Apart from a little excitement when we played *In the Mood* and some chaps in RAF uniform attempted to dance, we were pretty much ignored and we finished our set and began packing down. Well, I thought, that wasn't quite what I expected but I remembered the old adage: 'A gig's a gig!'

Just then a tall, good-looking chap came bounding up to me in immaculate evening dress.

"You chaps were amazing! Just what the Scene needs! All those dreadful cover bands like Chance, strumming away *So nice to see you*, ghaaastly! What are you called?" He said when he'd finished his air-guitar impersonation of the Chance Band.

I blinked. "Erm, well we haven't really got a name yet, we just got together for this one night."

"Really? Well, you must stay together, I've got a very smart party coming up, down the A303 somewhere, they would love you! Have you got a card?"

"Erm, no."

"You must get some and find a name for the band. Here's my card, come and see me on Monday and we can talk. Must dash I've got to work."

I looked at the card.

Angus Gibson Music
119-121 High St Kensington
London SW1

"Golly!" I said and showed it to the boys.

That weekend I was again invited up to Hampstead for one of the many lunches with Sir David and Lady S (Sandy). During drinks, Sandy introduced me to a tall chap, who reminded me of Peter O'Toole but I discovered that this was David Wynn, the sculptor. I was fortunate that having recently been filming in Wells Cathedral, I knew that he had been responsible for the highly controversial statue of Christ that had been placed high above the great West door facade of the Cathedral, replacing the original medieval one that had been all but destroyed by centuries of wind and rain. I knew he was also responsible for the fabulous *Boy with Dolphin* in bronze that was a landmark on the Chelsea Embankment by the Albert Bridge in front of a wine emporium called Balls Brothers. Other than that, I struggled in my knowledge of sculpture. Then a flash of inspiration!

Sir Thomas Beecham by David Wynn

"Do you know my favourite sculpture? It is in the Royal Festival Hall, as you go up the stairs. It's a bust of my great conducting hero, Sir Thomas Beecham with two very expressive hands. I don't know who did it, do you?"

"Ah yes, I should think so," he said, smiling, "that was one of mine, 1956, I believe…shall we go through to lunch?"

Lunch was served in the dining room with one of Sandy's paintings of Venice hanging where guests could enquire if it was a Canaletto. It really was very well executed, if not quite a masterpiece. Fiorenza piped up in a lull in the conversation:

"Daddy, guess what? Grimmy has just formed a Jazz Band!" Sir David glanced up from his Osso Bucco and you could see immediately that the burdensome thoughts regarding the Bank of England and the exchange rate mechanism and inflation, and all the fiscal and economic dilemmas of a City Bank director, just evaporated at this revelation.

"Really? You must tell me all about it."

David had been into jazz long before his talents as a financial whiz-kid were known and there were stories that he had played in smokey nightclubs with the talented singer Sandy Shaw in the 1960s. I told him the story of the Hammersmith Ball and he asked me what I proposed to call the band. Before I could answer, his face lit up into a huge smile.

"Graham and The Grahamophones!"

Everyone roared at this with cries of "brilliant" and "perfect".

I remained aloof and said that I wasn't sure that it was quite the worst name I had ever heard, to which he replied, that it was a shame as he would like to sponsor us to make a video. It was at that moment I realised without question that this was exactly the name I was looking for.

And so, for the next quarter of a century, I struggled with a name that was described by the radio presenter Adrian Love as the world's most musical typo. I also had to listen to BBC Radio 2's Derek Jameson splutter through his presentation of "The Gram...the Gra-Ham...the, the...oh get on with it Jameson!"

And it happened just like that. I contacted a prop hire company to get some lyre-shaped music stands and made overtures to a video company who advertised themselves as 'The Video Casting Directory'. I hired a new venue for the day in Shaftesbury Avenue and a whole gang of Fiorenza and Joey's very smart friends all turned up in 1920s costume, including a professional actor and a ballet dancer to be extras. We recorded about five numbers to video, including the Charleston and some 1930s numbers including the very amusing *She had to go and lose it at The Astor*, as made famous by Harry Roy. And there we were on the way to being Society's new favourite band. I still have a copy of the VHS with a cartoon of a '20s' couple in evening dress dancing and he is saying:

"Darling, I always think of you when I hear The Grahamophones play."

And she has a thought bubble which reads "I always think of Algy!"

The name was a difficult one for people to pronounce and it sometimes caused confusion. I had hired props from a theatrical warehouse in Edgware Road and was late paying them when the telephone rang. It was a broad Irish accent chasing an invoice:

"Oid loike to speak to Mr O'phones, please?"

"I'm sorry, who??"

"Mr Graham O'phones."

Sandy pulled strings with a good friend, Lotti Lewis (mother of Damian Lewis, the actor), who was the chairman on the Leukaemia League Ball Committee and got us booked to play at the Hurlingham Club. Sandy was seated next to Bruce Forsythe, who was the recipient of a sturdy kick under the table for daring to attempt to play footsie with our elegant sponsor. "Good game, good game!"

The video had very poor sound quality but visually it looked lovely. I had a message from Joey's mother that I must come to dinner as she wanted me to meet her German neighbour, Wolfgang, who had seen the video and loved the Charleston. I arrived in Parsons Green and was introduced to a man in his 80s with a splendid handlebar moustache and a charming smile. His energy and demeanour were incredible for a man of that age and, although his English was perfect, he had a studied, almost comical 'Tcherman Axcent'. He regaled us over dinner with tales of life in Berlin between the wars and the cabaret clubs and the dancing, particularly the Charleston, which he was eager to demonstrate to us after dinner. Then he played his ace card. He was part of a committee responsible for organising an annual ball in the Congresshalle in Berlin called the Tuntenball. They had already booked James Last and his Orchestra and Gloria (I will survive) Gaynor.

"Vould zer Gramaphonz be interested to come ant play ze Charleston at zis ball?"

I almost yelled Jawohl! Wow! This was an amazing offer and I had very little idea what to quote but he came up with a very decent package to include flights, food and accommodation. I relayed this to the boys who were as incredulous as I was.

We landed in Berlin and were transported to a lovely old-style hotel on the Kurfurstendamm where Wolfgang was waiting and saw to it that we had a good lunch with plenty of beer. During the soundcheck/rehearsal, we had only been going for ten minutes, when some of the boys began asking for a comfort break, having downed several litres of German beer. Rolling my eyes, I waved them away and off they all trooped to the Gents. Shortly after, one of them ran back asking what the German word for "Gents" was.

"Herren," I replied, "can you please get on with it!"

After five minutes, they all returned looking bemused and a little shocked.

"Bloody 'eck, Graham what's goin' on??"

I looked at my Yorkshire trumpet player quizzically.

"There are all these women in the gents' loo but they're not women; they're blokes in dresses and make-up and high heels!" Memories of Bangkok came flooding back and I turned round to Wolfgang for an explanation. He was laughing.

"But of course, I told you zis voz der Tuntenball!"

"Sorry Wolfgang but my German is limited. What does 'Tunten' mean?" I asked, pretty much guessing the reply by now.

"Tunte is German for Transvestite or cross-dresser and ve hav five sousand of zem coming tonight."

I turned to the brass section with a shrug and got the inevitable reply of "Bloody 'eck!"

We returned to England to sleep off our hangovers and prepare for our next event which was a posh country party down the A303 somewhere. It was the sort of party where you arrive and have a glass of champagne and Guinness, a 'Black Russian' shoved in your hand. The 'Lord of the Manor', as it were, was proper Old Money, and could probably trace his ancestry back to the Norman Conquest. Angus had set up his disco and I had the band all set and ready by six o'clock on a glorious Summer's evening in Dorset when our genial host ambled up to us and asked us if we needed anything and to help ourselves to drinks. He then said, "I expect you chaps need to get yourselves all pumped up, don't you? What do you do, shove some powder up your nose or something?"

He was clearly under the illusion that all musicians had a cocaine habit. Mind you, in the 1930s, he wouldn't have been so far wrong, Louis Armstrong being a famous example.

1986 was a big year for the orchestra and perhaps, because of its initial rapid success, tensions amongst young musicians began to emerge with each new success. I wanted to take on a management company and work on our publicity, our repertoire and our style. I was looking to pursue the not very commercial lane of recreating an English dance band, like that of Lew Stone or Ambrose, playing English arrangements of English and American repertoire. Then I struck gold. In Charlotte Street, in London, the BBC had buried about five thousand stock dance band arrangements (presumably to keep them safe during the Blitz) and the librarian there was pleased with my interest in this collection. He agreed to photocopy some of these arrangements for a fee and allowed me to spend several weeks in this basement going through the dusty bags of music. Then came a much-needed breakthrough. An agent in Germany had been at the Tuntenball and contacted me to offer us five weeks work. It was a Silja Line Ship, top of the range, and we were to play music for dancing every night for five weeks. The boat would sail from Stockholm to Åbo (Turku), the old capital of Finland. The restaurant was five star with a bar above and a balcony overlooking the ballroom with two sweeping staircases onto the ballroom floor. Behind the orchestra was a huge panoramic window at the very bow of the ship, which was travelling pretty quickly through the Baltic waters, through a great number of tiny rocky islands, each of which had a light on it. The ship was piloted by computer so it could move quickly and the scene to the passengers was like that of the Starship Enterprise in that it really did look like you were travelling through space with the islands like stars flashing past on either side and ahead.

During this time, the BBC posted out more arrangements of songs by Irving Berlin, Cole Porter and Rogers and Hart. The great thing was that both the Swedes and the Finns were all proper dancers which they had been taught at school. So, they all knew how to Foxtrot, Quickstep and Jive. The drawback was that the Finns absolutely adored the Tango and the Waltz which is not standard repertoire for a swing orchestra. Notwithstanding, we endured the gruelling schedule and returned to London as tight a musical ensemble as you could imagine with a full repertoire of authentic 1930s arrangements.

On returning to London, I had a meeting with Angus Gibson to learn that in the winter months he wasn't really able to fix the band any work, and as he wished to go into sound installations, we agreed to part company. He was, I know, very tied up with a contract for Edward Heath to install a speaker system in every room at Arundels, his Salisbury residence. I went from a smart Kensington office to a small cottage business called NDS Management in Isleworth. A piano playing, ex-schoolteacher, called Dave, who ran a jazz band called The 'New Dixie Syncopators' with his partner Marion, made up the company. But they were keen and worked very hard to try to fix us work. The problem was that, at first, all they could manage was a pub gig at the Half Moon in Putney every Wednesday. This was good to invite people who might want to hear the band before booking. Our demo tape then was very primitive. Sure enough, after a few weeks, Dave Lovatt, the brother of our trumpet Mike Lovatt, brought down a colleague from the BBC where he worked. His name was Russell England, a producer. At the end of the evening, I was asked if I would be interested in making a documentary for BBC Television. Crikey!

Several weeks earlier, I had been to see a record company, who David and Marion knew, in an attempt to get a record deal. David Kassner, the son, had been to hear us at the pub, seen the packed crowd and was suitably impressed enough to inform his father Edward Kassner. The record company were called President Records, which was really a front for their music publishing company, 'Kassner President'. The deal was as tough a one as you could imagine. There would be no money for the recording artists but they would pay for the producer, the studio, the pressing and the marketing cost including a plugger. On top of that, we would need to write two original songs for the album of which Kassner President would own the rights.

Edward Kassner was a diminutive character, clearly Jewish, with a strong Austrian accent, who had cheated the Nazis of their prey and fled to Holland where he had hidden among the dykes before fleeing via a fishing boat to England in 1939. Both his parents perished in Auswichtz. But he was a survivor and began song writing in 1946 with a hit for Vera Lynn *How Lucky You Are*. His publishing company had some big hits too, including *Rock around the clock* and by the time I met him, he was near to retirement but still sat behind a huge desk sporting a Churchillian cigar. I was seated on a very low chair so I was not in a good negotiating position but he was amusing; his catchphrase being "Do you vont coffees or do you vont a career?" meaning this was a no-frills deal and that he was doing me a favour by taking me on. I signed.

The next problem I had was that I had never written a song let alone scored for one. Night after night I sweated over a tune that was a sort of syncopated inversion of *I Got Rhythm* by Gershwin. I scored it for three saxes, three brass, obligato violin and rhythm. The lyrics were daft but tongue in cheek. It was called *I'd Sooner Be a Crooner* and the lyrics were as follows:

I would Sooner Be a Crooner given half a chance
I come complete with two left feet for dancing
I'm well aware that Fred Astaire could sing as well as dance
But partners flee when they see me advancing
Now across a crowded room I wouldn't dance, I'd only croon
Trotting out those quick, quick slows, pounding away right on her toes
You may trip the light fantastic, take your partner's hand,
I'd sooner be a crooner in a band!

We recorded it at PYE studio near Marble Arch with the rest of the album. The title track was *We're Tops on Saturday Night*, as played by Ambrose but it was my song that got released as a single and pushed by the radio plugger. Edward Kassner loved it and would always say:

"Grrr-raham! Write me more Crrr-ooners!"

It was amazing to be driving along with the radio on and hear your voice and your music suddenly come over the airwaves. I even heard it coming from a radio from a building site! Sir David bought a box of 50 LPs and gave them out in the City and a party planner, Jonathan Seaward of 'Joffins' fame, who had just opened a record shop in Parsons Green, was astonished enough to phone me up with the news that our album was his shop's biggest seller and they had re-ordered.

Over the Autumn and the following Winter, I began filming for the BBC and it was decided that the programme was to be called *I'd Sooner Be a Crooner*. The crew came to the Half Moon in Putney to film a packed pub cheering and singing along with the *Chinese Laundry Blues*, "Oh Mr Wu!" A week later, we had organised a dance at 'The Waldorf' and the band were filmed there with everyone dressed to the nines and the band performing *Life Begins at Oxford Circus* and *A Nightingale Sang in Berkeley Square*. The film is only 40 minutes long but it includes some wonderful vintage footage of Henry Hall and the BBC Dance Orchestra, Carroll Gibbons, Al Bowlly, Harry Roy, Ambrose and a clever sequence where I am singing *A Nightingale Sang* and it fades into an anti-aircraft battery and original footage of the Blitz, as only the BBC would have access to.

The film went out on a Friday night at peak viewing time of 7:30 and got rave reviews from all the newspapers. "Real instruments, real singing, real style" (The Times) with the glaring exception of one waspish writer from The Independent: "Dalby is very full of himself and has absolutely nothing to croon about, his voice is bland and lacks tone"…who then goes on to make the film pick of the evening's viewing! I remember at the time being quite hurt by the personal nature of the attack on what was and is a really interesting short film, but then it was *only* the Independent struggling to be different. It's on You Tube but the transfer is from an old VHS so the quality is average. The final scene was shot in the Orangery at Holland Park with a camera on a rail track. The doors are all open, it was early January and I was trying to look cool when actually, I was freezing! When the credits come up, I always spare a thought for the charming Dave Lovatt who helped get the band this fantastic opportunity; he was lost to us tragically young.

The impact was immediate. We landed two international bookings and one for Lady Aberdeen, in Scotland. The others were jazz festivals; Alphen in Holland and Molde in Norway. The first was to travel to Scotland by train which took forever. We were collected at Edinburgh station by an aged retainer and driven the one-hour journey to Haddo House, where Lady Aberdeen was throwing a ball for the great and good in the area. Whilst the band was being shown their quarters, I was ushered into the large drawing-room to meet the lady of the house and her charming son. He mentioned that they had enjoyed seeing us on television and thought it would be nice to have some '30s' dance band music for a change, as the locals only ever had Scottish Jigs and Reels. He said however much they demanded an Eightsome Reel or a Strathspey we were to stick to our repertoire. That made sense to me as I had no idea how to play a Strathspey or even what it was! The dancing started off all right with people foxtrotting and the like but after half an hour, requests started to come in for Scottish dancing, which I politely refused. After 45 minutes, a red-face woman, reeking of whiskey, practically fell onto the stage to tell me her opinion of our music concluding with a slurred:

"It's ourrrrr herrrritage!"

A good time to take a break. I followed the band off on their rapid journey to the bar when I was stopped by a butler.

"Excuse me, sir, therrre's a young lassie who'd like a woorrrd wi'ye."

He pointed to a table in the corner of the marquee where there was indeed a 'lassie' with short, spiky blond hair and a rather angular, intelligent face. I sighed as I guessed she was going to request music that wasn't dance band swing but was pleasantly surprised when she shook my hand without giving her name and announced:

"I like your music."

Well, that broke the ice, and soon I was to discover that she was, in fact, a singer-songwriter herself and had been to the Guildhall to study music. I asked her how her career was progressing and if she got many gigs, to which she replied that it wasn't too bad. I sympathised and agreed that it was hard when you first start out. I said I needed to get a drink before the next set and rose to leave. At this, she said, "Oh, before you go, can you tell me the title of that last song you played, I really liked the tune." I gave her the title *Keep Young and Beautiful* (If you want to be loved) and she wrote it down on a notepad she had produced from her handbag. We exchanged pleasantries and I tootled off to join the boys at the bar.

"What was she like?" asked a sax player.

"I've no idea who she was but she's a singer and she's one of the few here who like our music," I said.

At this, he burst out laughing. "That was Annie Lennox!!"

Oh, dear God, and I asked her if she got many gigs. Aaaargh!!

Two years later, she released another international, best-selling album of which the final track was her take on *Keep Young and Beautiful*.

The Molde Jazz Festival was not one I had heard of but what a wow it turned out to be. We played in this beautiful hotel by a fjord so that when you opened your balcony window you got a perfect mirror image of the snow-capped mountains.

The Grahamophones at the Waldorf for our first album for President Records in 1986

I befriended an American guy, who turned out to be the lead singer with Manhattan Transfer, and he said that Miles Davis was in the room down the corridor! We talked about singing, and the road manager who was with me, said that he had overheard some of my musicians, particularly the drummer and the guitarist, having a really good rant about me behind my back. This confirmed some suspicions I already had concerning the ambitions of the drummer and the recently appointed guitar/banjo player who, unlike the rest of us, was an elderly, cynical veteran of the music business. There was a full-on takeover plot afoot and I was about to be given the stab in the back treatment so favoured by Brutus and Cassius. The concerts in Norway were a great success and the band then was as tight as it had ever been. But this was to be the last time we ever played together.

Chapter 17
The Night of the Long Knives

I returned to England with the band and could not fail to notice that there was a discernible shiftiness about the musicians in their attitude towards me, and reluctance to speak to me or look me in the eye. It was as if they were planning to rob me or something. I spoke to my agents about this who had also heard from the road manager working for the John Boddy Agency, who had booked us in Norway, that there was indeed dirty work afoot. It was difficult as some really high-quality work was just starting to come in.

An eccentric lawyer called Elizabeth Wolfe had got us a job in Hong Kong, just prior to Norway, for practically no money but it was, as she put it, a sprat to catch a mackerel. We played in some hotel or other for some charity or other but Elizabeth was indefatigable in getting us marketed out there and known to her Hong Kong chums, who included Gilbert Rodway QC, who was close buddies with Derek Nimmo and Leslie Phillips. They would pop out from time to time to perform plays and comedies and bring some big-name English actors out for a working holiday. So, out of this connection, came an invite to perform at The Hong Kong International Arts Festival. This also coincided with an invite to perform for a charity very close to my heart (literally), The Great Ormond Street Hospital charity ball in Dubai. Not only this but an Italian chum of Fiorenza's, the debonair Carlo Ducci, who was a journalist for Vogue Magazine in Milan, had mentioned to his bad-boy skiing friend, the Italian champion Alberto Tomba, who loved swing music, that he knew someone called 'Grimmy' who had this fantastic orchestra. So, you see, this was a very bad time indeed to be changing horses.

I heard down the grapevine that the veteran, scheming guitarist had arranged with the ambitious drummer to call a meeting of the 'Bruvvers' at his house to discuss the details of the assassination plot. I was presented with this extraordinarily written ultimatum the following day:

"The members of the Band formally (sic) known as The Grahamophones have met and have unanimously voted on the following changes to be made:

That Graham Dalby relinquish his title and duties as Band Leader and that from now on the band will be run as a co-operative and that all decisions will be decided on by a majority vote by its members.

That the name of the band will no longer be Graham Dalby and The Grahamophones and that a temporary title of The Gramophones be adopted until the members have voted on a new name.

The members agree to allow Graham Dalby to remain in recognition of his work in getting gigs and paying for the music but he must only appear as a singer and when not singing must sit at the side of the stage.

All count-ins must be done by the drummer and presentations done by the guitarist.

If Graham Dalby is not agreeable to this the band will continue as above but with a female vocalist.

I felt like Tsar Nicholas II! I sat up through the night, with my newlywed wife (Susanne-née Engström, whom I had met in Finland and had come to live in London), with several bottles of wine, trying to work this one through. I was over a barrel insofar as my trust in them had been such that they all looked after their own music, without which I couldn't operate as no copies had yet been made. I had a concert to perform in Cologne the following Saturday for the Italian 'Tomba' set. My feelings of betrayal were submerged by my instinct for survival. I had created this band out of nothing and we had come so far so quickly. I recalled the talk in my hotel room, with the road manager and the lead singer of Manhattan Transfer, who had convinced me that I was the named artist and that all musicians were, therefore, replaceable. My management company were equally supportive. The musicians thought it was they who were the booking attraction. It turned out not to be so. That night Susanne convinced me that the only answer was to be as ruthless as the aspiring usurpers and we agreed that we would sack the lot and start afresh with a clean sheet.

The following day, I informed my management company of my decision, and they whole-heartedly concurred. I spent the day on the telephone to all the four music conservatories and to various other musicians that I knew. By an odd stroke of irony, the ninja-assassin drummer in the band had recently been unable to make one of the gigs and had booked a young, talented, good-looking and incredibly enthusiastic drummer who had just left the Royal Marines. When I told him I was looking to audition a new band, he couldn't believe his luck. Within an hour, he had lined up a bassist, a guitarist and a piano player who had been in the RM Band as pianist to The Queen Mother aboard the Royal Yacht Britannia. The drummer still plays with us today and the pianist is a top MD who I still get to do arrangements for us. Brass players and sax players turned up from The Royal Academy, Trinity and Guildhall and I had no trouble whatsoever filling the places. The management company contacted the musicians of the coup demanding the immediate return of the music if they wished to be paid for any outstanding work. All the music was returned and all the renegade musicians paid. A day later a leaflet arrived, sent to The John Boddy Agency, of a hastily prepared photo of my erstwhile orchestra that must have been taken before my ultimatum was presented. It was taken at the Pagoda in Battersea Park and included a girl singer who I had never seen before or since. It read something like: 'The Mayfair Radio Orchestra formally (sic) known as The Gramophones (sic) are now accepting bookings with their fabulous new vocalist, Triksy Bubbles'. (No, I made up that last bit!). My management was furious and got a lawyer onto it right away as 'passing off' and forced the withdrawal of that pamphlet.

The air tickets were changed for a small fee and my new band met at the Half Moon, Putney, to rehearse all the material. To be fair, they were not yet as tight as the previous team but they were all delighted to have the work and incredulous when I talked about Dubai, Hong Kong and a forthcoming album with President Records. The Cologne event went off well but I returned to London to some rather worrying news. The BBC had booked us to play at a ball at the Savoy for Children in Need but there had been a message to call them as they wished to cancel. When I phoned the producer, he was very apologetic but said that an identical band had offered to do the job for nothing and that, being a charity, it was his duty to accept...unless I could also offer my band for free. Well, I wasn't going down that road. I suggested that he take the very generous offer and asked for the name of the band. The Mayfair Radio...yes, yes...I guessed that much. My record company took a table near the stage and I enjoyed sitting there, being waited on, and sipping Savoy champagne whilst talking loudly with BBC producers about our forthcoming album and exciting foreign tours. All this as the musicians on stage sweated away for no remuneration. In the break, the trombonist came up to me and begged me to put the band back together as it was. I noticed that neither of my trumpet players, Mike or John was present. No, sadly, it was too late for that.

In another act of attempted sabotage, the agent for the Hong Kong Arts Festival said he had been contacted by some 'old jazzer' (the scheming guitarist) to say that Graham Dalby and The Grahamophones no longer existed but that most of the musicians were available to play at the festival under the name of the Mayfair Radio Orchestra. I assured the agent that, not only had we just returned from a successful trip to Germany but that we were about to record a new album. His words were 'as long as you are there at the front of a good orchestra with your name on it, I don't care who plays'. That said it all and I never felt threatened or troubled by that particular group again. They split up shortly afterwards as the brass players went their own ways with the trumpet player, Mike Lovatt, joining me for the second album. Apparently, he was called a 'traitor' by the hard-core militants. Crisis averted, onwards and upwards...phew!

Chapter 18
Loyalty Rewarded

February in the music business can be a bit quiet so it was wonderful to be offered two weeks work, in what was to be, one of the best paid holidays of my career. Having calmed the jitters of the Hong Kong Arts Festival Director, we set to work recording a second album with President Records called Mad Dogs and Englishmen. It was a much softer sound than the previous album and concentrated on English music from 1935 to 1940. My tenor chum from Trinity, Andy Busher, had joined 'The Swingle Singers' and, as a result, I became good friends with a number of them, including the arranger, Jonathan Rathbone. His arrangements for the Swingles were brilliant and based on this, I commissioned him to create an arrangement of Mad Dogs and Englishmen. What he came up with was inspired and I posed for the front cover in a leather armchair with my own Mad Dog called Grub from Battersea Dogs Home. It was released on vinyl, cassette and, for the first time, Compact Disc. Now we had something pretty decent to take to Hong Kong.

Before we flew to Hong Kong, we had a week-long stopover in Dubai to perform at some fundraising events on behalf of the Great Ormond Street Children's Hospital Appeal; the same hospital that had saved my life after my hasty evacuation from Africa in 1958. We were sponsored by BritishAirways and flew Business Class to Dubai, where we were shown lavish hospitality and treated like stars. On one free day, we were all taken out into the desert for a photoshoot in two air-conditioned Land-cruisers, packed full of food and cold beer. We changed into our black-tie gear for about 15 minutes to get the photoshoot over as quickly as possible in the fierce desert sun before getting back into shorts, t-shirts and flip-flops. The photos were fabulous (see back page)! We were then driven to a shaded oasis where the guides prepared a traditional Arabic lunch of lamb cooked over a fire, shaded by some palm trees.

Our 2nd Album with President Records 1988

The photos were fabulous (see back page)! We were then driven to a shaded oasis where the guides prepared a traditional Arabic lunch of lamb cooked over a fire, shaded by some palm trees. Then, to our great surprise, out came a chocolate birthday cake from the vehicle's fridge, complete with candles and chilled champagne. They had noticed from our DOBs on our passports that one of our young saxophone players, Phil Whelan, was celebrating his 21st birthday on that very day. A day he will never forget.

We arrived in Hong Kong looking dreadful. The final night party in Dubai had been quite a session and the boys slept for most of the flight. We were mostly unshaven and looked like so many hobos rather than an international swing orchestra arriving at a major international festival. Topping the bill was André Previn with the Vienna Philharmonic Orchestra. We were driven to the Hei-dun Jau Dim, the Hong Kong Hilton, which boasted the famous Dragon Boat Bar as featured in John le Carré's novel, 'The Honourable Schoolboy'. The boys in the band were incredulous to hear me chatting to the driver in Cantonese and soon we arrived in our dishevelled state. We were greeted by a member of the hotel staff and a representative of the Hong Kong Arts festival who said they had arranged a reception for us. I was horrified at the thought of press and photographers seeing us at far less than our best but was put at my ease when it turned out to be only us and white-jacketed waiters bearing silver trays of ice-cold champagne and dim sum. Remembering back to my first arrival in Hong Kong and the exertions we were put through, I smiled to myself, pleased to be back and pleased to not have someone screaming at me to "drop and give me twenty" but rather topping up my glass with Veuve Cliquot. This, I felt, was the life.

That evening, as it was our first wedding anniversary, I let the boys go out to play in Hong Kong whilst my wife and I dined in the lovely restaurant in the hotel. We didn't stint ourselves and enjoyed lobster, lovely wine and a delicious dessert. I had mentioned to a chatty waiter that it was our anniversary and two glasses of champagne arrived with sparklers and everyone clapped. The big shock came when I called for the *mai-dan* (the bill) and the manager came up and said "m-sai bei chin". My wife looked at my shocked face.

"What did he say?"

I explained that the manager had said the whole fabulous dinner was 'on the house'!

"Doh-je! Doh-je!" I said with great relief as the bill was looking to be a substantial one. We returned to our room but the night was still young, so I suggested we go for a little sightseeing. I hailed a cab and asked him to take us up to the Peak, the highest point in Hong Kong where the views are breath-taking. We took with us the complimentary bottle of cognac that we found amid the orchids in our room. The taxi left us at a deserted spot at the top of the Peak near a Chinese temple structure with no walls. From there, we could look at the incredible neon vista below, from Hong Kong harbour, right across to Kowloon and beyond, to the dark shadows of the New Territories. Below, in the harbour, the little Star Ferries passed each other working, indefatigably, through the night. I was in high spirits, what with the dinner and the cognac, and the roof of the little temple echoed and amplified my laughter. I think it was at this point that the Chinese gods felt they'd had enough of this gweiloh! On a warm and humid night, there suddenly came a rustling of branches and out of nowhere, came cold, powerful gusts of wind. My wife and I simultaneously felt a strong urge to get out of that place, though no words were spoken. It was like being pushed out by an unseen force. We both walked quickly along the road giggling nervously when, right above me, came a loud crack and I ran forward at a sprint. Not a second too soon, a large branch from a tree came hurtling down to the spot where I had been walking. We both ran down the hill as fast as we could until I turned around to check that what I thought had happened had, in fact, actually happened.

We both burst out laughing with more than a touch of hysteria and incredulity. There were no taxis up at The Peak at that time of night so there was nothing for it but to start the long descent on foot. By the time we approached the hotel, it was sunrise and we watched, fascinated, the early risers performing their slow-motion martial art warm-up known as Tai chi.

We reached our room at about 5:30 am and collapsed into bed exhausted. After just a few hours, the telephone by my bed rang loudly and jolted me out of a dreamless sleep.

"Ahh, Mister Dahbee?" enquired a female voice.

"Huur? Mmm? Whaaa?" I replied. Then, my memory came back and I remembered that I had agreed to give a radio interview for RTHK at 9:00am. I forced myself awake as I was put through to a loud, brash transatlantic accent:

"Hi, I'm Dave!"

We exchanged pleasantries and he played a track from our first album and I chatted in a voice that sounded as though I smoked 40 a day. Then came the crunch question:

"So, Graham, what would you say if I said that some people might think that your band is just a copy of the Pasadena Roof Orchestra?"

"I would say that neither you nor some people understand much about music. We are playing from original arrangements from the 30s period whilst the other band are more 20s-style Dixie-based, using more jazz improvisations and, actually, what would André Previn say if you suggested to him that the Vienna Philharmonic were just a copy of the Berlin Philharmonic...hmm?" There was a pause.

"Well, you can hear Graham Dalby and his great band at the Hilton Hotel as part of the Hong Kong Arts Festival," etc. and he cut to music. I was furious!

"Guess I riled you, huh?"

"Yes, Dave, I guess you did, well done!"

The events in Hong Kong went very well and the great and good from Hong Kong Society all turned out to support us. It was here that I met an Australian lawyer called Ted Marr, who knew absolutely everybody and gushed about our music. He was to play an important part in my future trips to the Far East and saw to it that everyone in Hong Kong knew all about me and the band.

Chapter 19
First Encounter with Royalty

On returning to England, I had a number of engagements to fulfil. One came in at surprisingly short notice, considering it was a major society party, thrown by the Duke and Duchess of Devonshire at Chatsworth House. We arrived at Chatsworth after a long hot drive and were taken to the house to set up. I looked around at the sheer size and splendour and was sad that I didn't have my A team with me, rather a scratch team got together at short notice. What I did have, though, was an Essex bass player with an attitude and a mouth to match. His name was Tony who was a character and, despite being adopted, had traced his father, many years later, to Venice.

We were billeted at a large cottage nearby where we watched England being knocked out by Germany in the World Cup, during a penalty shootout, of course! At 8:00pm, the guests started to arrive in droves and were mini-bussed up to the double staircase to be greeted by the Duchess, the youngest of the Mitford sisters, herself. I heard an amusing story that the then Texan wife of Mick Jagger, Jerry Hall, had not received an invitation so thought she would turn up anyway. At the top of the stairs, the Duchess greeted her with the welcoming remark:

"How very clever of you to discover I was having a little soirée…"

At 10:00pm, we made our way up to the House and watched the most extravagant firework and laser display over the lake. When it all died down we began to play in the quadrangle of Chatsworth. Some people danced but there were many other bands and entertainments going on. After a long set, we reached 1:00 a.m. and I finally turned to the boys and thanked them. It was a warm and still night and I retired into a small room nearby to have a cooling drink when one of my musicians rushed into the room saying there was a bit of a crisis. It appeared that the band who were booked to replace us had not turned up and someone was trying very hard to persuade my tired musicians to continue playing. By the time

I had re-tied my bow tie and returned to the fray, it was all over and the band were all assembled back on the stage. It appeared that Viscount Linley had tried to get the band to continue playing. Tony had appointed himself shop-steward and declared it would have to be a 'shedload of extra dosh'. The good Viscount had taken out his chequebook and pen and said to the band, "How much?"
Tony had replied, "Nah, mate…might bounce. Gotta be cash, two big ones!"

The elderly Duke was sent for and the safe opened. A cluster of £50 note bundles were placed onto the piano in a vulgar display and the band struck up, totally revived, as if by a miracle. I was mortified with embarrassment. We continued to play into the night, notching up nearly five hours of music. Finally, at 3.00 am, we came, mercifully, to a halt. I noticed a cluster of princesses all sporting glittering tiaras and from thence, came a diminutive figure, clutching a whiskey glass, with a cigarette in her elegant, black-gloved hand. She came right up to the stage and I recognised her as Princess Margaret and made a little appropriate bow. She smiled up and said, "I hear you've played on for twice as long because the other band didn't arrive and I think you are absolutely marvellous. I shall mention you to my sister, the Queen."
I smiled and nodded, thinking, *Oh yes…and you are so going to remember that in the morning?*

And so it was that, some three months later, there was a knock at the door from a curious postman who wanted to deliver a letter in person as it carried the Royal Crest. He wondered if I'd been awarded an MBE or something. I fetched a knife and opened the letter carefully.

Dear Mr Dalby

Her Majesty, the Queen has asked me to write to you and say that she would be very pleased, if you are available, to play music for dancing at Buckingham Palace on December 10th. You may be pleased to know that you came to Her Majesty's attention via a recommendation from the Princess Margaret.
Please contact me at my office to discuss what you need.

Yours Sincerely

Lt Col. Blair Stewart-Wilson OBE
Master of the Queen's Household

"Wow! Well, I've made someone's day," said the postman, as he continued on his way.

I shook my head incredulously and said aloud to myself, "so you did remember, you darling lady!"

The plans for the Ball proceeded with me being asked to the Palace to meet the Master of the Household and generally get a full briefing. It was explained that the party was for the four Royal Birthdays; The Queen Mother had reached 90, Princess Margaret 60, Princess Anne 40 and Prince Andrew 30. It was to be a family and friends' event without dignitaries from around the world spoiling it. The Queen, always shrewdly careful about expenditure, had come up with a brilliant idea; those guests living in Central London would each host a house party and lay on a dinner for those guests who lived outside London. All the guests could then, having been fed, decant to Buckingham Palace for dancing and a glass of Blue Nun or similar at 10:30pm and be offered breakfast from 1:30am.

And so it was that I found myself leading a Swing Band, in the long gallery at Buckingham Palace, with Princess Diana urging us to get on with it, even though most of the guests hadn't yet arrived. We struck up a lively tune, *Jeepers Creepers*, I think, and Princess Diana leapt onto the dance floor dragging some poor old chap practically off his feet. She was a picture of youthful exuberance in a stunning midnight blue, off the shoulder, ballgown, highlighting her beautifully coiffured blond hair and some very expensive-looking diamonds adorning her shapely and sun-tanned shoulders. It was December! Nobody in the room could resist the whoop of encouragement she gave and very soon the dance floor was full.

The evening passed off smoothly and we were followed by a pop covers band, none other than The Chance Band, so nicely sent up by Angus Gibson at the Hammersmith Palais. The hospitable Master of the Household invited me to stay on and join the party adding that he would introduce me to some of the guests. There were an assortment of actors, sportsmen and women and I recognised a few: Jackie Stewart the racing driver, Willie Carson the jockey and Anthony Andrews the actor. It was here that the Colonel stopped and said, "Ah, let me introduce you to Prince Andrew. Your Royal Highness, may I introduce you to Mr Graham Dalby?"

Considering I had just been standing on a stage fronting a 14-piece swing orchestra in a hard-to-miss white dinner jacket, the 'who the devil are you then' attitude that the Prince adopted took me somewhat aback. I was about to retort with some ill-advised witty repost when I was saved, in the nick of time, by the intervention of the wonderful Anthony Andrews.

"Aren't you the same chap who played for my wife's charity do at St James' the other day?"

"Oh yes!" I rejoined, relieved that an awkward moment had been averted. Apparently, Mrs Andrews had been delighted.

I wasn't to see Anthony Andrews again for a long time but in October 2002, I was singing at a charity concert in The Royal Albert Hall with some big stars, including Roger Waters from Pink Floyd and the Royal Philharmonic Orchestra. Jeremy Irons and Anthony Andrews were doing a sort of Ant and Dec double act, announcing people on and Anthony Andrews called me onto the stage where I performed a Sinatra number before a packed audience. I think they originally wanted Robbie Williams as I was told which song I should sing *Have You Met Miss Jones* but he was clearly not available, so I let it rip!

Back at the palace, I moved swiftly away from the Duke of York's set, only to be thumped robustly between the shoulder blades by the heartiest of princesses as if I had just completed a clear round. I turned and there was the jolly aspect of the Princess Royal who complimented me on the music and was pleased we had played her grandmother's favourite, *A Nightingale Sang in Berkeley Square*. Princess Anne was very affable and easy to get on with and had that same gift, of putting you at your ease and taking an interest in what you do, that I discovered in her brother, The Prince of Wales, when I met him some years later at the Guards chapel on his birthday. I must say though, at no time did I see Prince Charles at that party. Diana arrived with the Duchess of York surprising my wife, (who was having a sneaky smoke on the backstairs) by coming up that way for a surprise entrance. Breakfast was served in the throne room in the early hours and included the most delicious kedgeree I have ever tasted. It was bizarre to be standing up in this red plush, high-ceilinged room, eating kedgeree with a fork, just six feet away from the throne of England. It was getting late and I was thinking about slipping away when I thought I ought to try and see if I could find Princess Margaret and thank her for ensuring that we were a part of this amazing evening.

I had expected to find the princess surrounded by a crowd of her friends, holding sway and being witty and clever. But it was late and the throng had thinned out as people took their leave and I was surprised to be confronted with a sort of apparition. Princess Margaret was standing by a long window in a corner quite alone, in the pale light of a winter moon, shimmering on her pale-peach silk ball gown. She was gazing wistfully at the freezing paparazzi outside, desperate for a story from the departing guests, so had her back to me. I made a little cough, in the style of Jeeves and opened the conversation.

"Ahem, excuse me Your Royal Highness but I am the band leader who played at Chatsworth and whom you so kindly recommended to play here with my orchestra this evening, I just wished to thank you."

She looked at me with wide-eyed astonishment at my effrontery for having addressed a senior Royal without having been spoken to first, as is the protocol. She signalled to a flunky, not to have me removed but to stub out a dying cigarette and her face softened as he lit the replacement she had inserted into her cigarette holder.

"Oh yes, I remember, at the Devonshire's party…your people played half the night as the other band didn't show up. Yes, we all thought it was a valiant effort and I mentioned this to my sister, the Queen and well, here you are! I am so pleased."

She smiled and I smiled and mumbled some more thanks as she turned to the window to indicate the audience was over. The flunky nodded at me as if to say "that's your lot mate, now off you trot and don't be speaking to royals again without being asked to". I withdrew leaving the diminutive figure silhouetted in the moonlight once more. I thought she cut a sad and lonely figure but I was so pleased to have managed to thank her in person. It was only later that I read up on how troubled her life had been, with the great disappointments her position had created in her private life. But she loved music and was herself an accomplished pianist, so I felt fortunate that she had been there that night to notice us. I had been briefed that under no

circumstances should I speak to the press about this private party. Therefore, at about three in the morning, I slipped out the back way from the Royal Mews, avoiding the shivering press who were desperately snapping every car that left through the Palace front gates.

I awoke the next morning and rushed out to get the papers. As there was no information available to them, most just gave it a few lines and had a nice Palace publicity photograph of the 'Four Royals' in a group with the Queen Mother, seated. All, except the Daily Mail which I read in absolute astonishment! The headline: 'Elton John Entertains Royals at Palace Bash with sing along around the piano'. Whaaat?? I had been there from start to finish and could testify that Elton John was certainly not there. He would definitely not have been to the taste of Princess Margaret nor The Queen Mother's. Princess Diana would have approved but it was not her party. Who had fed the Mail this story? I never found out but the next day, a full apology was published by an embarrassed editor and an outraged letter from Elton John's management saying that he was currently in the United States and had not received an invitation. Ha! My orchestra and I, however, remained anonymous as the real orchestra who had played that night. A once in a lifetime experience had just happened and I knew that unless the Queen Mother made it to 100, it was unlikely to happen again and even if it did, what were the chances of getting booked twice...?

Chapter 20
The Baltic Sea – 1991 Viking Line

The fact that the party at Buckingham Palace went ahead in December 1990 was a great relief to me and the band, as there was a very real prospect of it being cancelled given that Britain was on the brink of war. On 2nd August, 1990, Saddam Hussein, without any declaration of war, invaded Kuwait, occupied the country and seized its, not inconsiderable, assets including its oilfields. The fact that the party went ahead was a clear indication to me that nothing would happen until the New Year, particularly as we had a new Prime Minister who had nothing like the metal of his recently ousted predecessor Mrs Thatcher, dubbed the 'Iron Lady'. The tension in the Middle East had been brewing for some time as Iraq was in great financial difficulty resulting from the cost of the Iran-Iraq War 1980-1988. Most of Iraq's debt was owed to Saudi Arabia and because the UAE and Kuwait had been exceeding OPEC quotas on oil production, prices had slumped from $18 a barrel to $10 a barrel which caused a loss to Iraq of some $7 billion a year; the equivalent of its balance of payments deficit in 1989. The Iraqi government described it as economic warfare. Iraq demanded $10 billion from Kuwait, Kuwait offered $500 million and Iraq, with the fourth largest army in the world, invaded. The Kuwaiti military, numbering just 16,000, stood for less than two days with just enough time to get the royal family out and to safety. The US government had at first been of a mind that it was a fait accompli but Mrs Thatcher reminded US President George Bush that appeasement with Saddam Hussain would leave the Gulf at his mercy, along with 65% of the world's oil supply. Appeasement with Hitler had been disastrous and recent dealings with Argentina's General Gualtieri had, likewise, not responded to diplomacy. She urged the US president "not to go wobbly". By the time John Major took over as the new Prime Minister, Britain was fully committed to the invasion of Kuwait and Iraq in January 1991.

It was against this dramatic global backdrop that I found myself in, of all places, a floating gin palace travelling from Stockholm to Turku (the ancient Viking capital of Finland). The Viking Line was, indeed, a ferry but more than that, it was a pleasure cruise that enabled Finns and Swedes to let off steam during a 12-hour journey and eat and drink themselves silly with the duty-free prices, fine restaurants and a British dance band who had taken a six-week contract to play four 45-minute sets a day. There were no gigs in the UK because of the Gulf crisis so this seemed like a good idea at the time. Wrong! This was one of the most mind-numbing things I have ever done in my life. Worse, the band, although made up of fantastic players, took to drinking on stage and the standard of playing wasn't great. I told the band there was to be no more alcohol on stage. (I later discovered that the large jugs of orange juice that the boys were drinking were heavily laced with vodka!) After we finished our last set, the boys would go upstairs to the disco which was packed with beautiful, young, drunk Finnish and Swedish girls, who were delighted to make the acquaintance of young English musicians. As I had my Finland/Swedish wife on board with me, I was exempt from these temptations. The great fascination for me was to listen to the radio and hear the unfolding of 'The Mother of All Wars', as Saddam described it.

One evening, we went to the public cafeteria on the boat for a late-night snack. There was a bit of a queue from people who had come down from the disco and who were chatting and laughing and generally enjoying themselves. All seemed well. An elderly security guard stood by watching sleepily. Behind me, I heard the unmistakeable staccato of a harsh, Glaswegian accent:

"R-Yooo Anglish?"

I turned around and said that I was but that my wife was a Finland-Swede. He then railed on about how 'roood' the Finns were and how his friend was currently looking for a Finn who had barged into him in the bar and what he was going to do to him. I immediately sensed that there was a situation developing and my instincts were confirmed when a large Finn came charging into the cafeteria, knocking over tables, hotly pursued by a Scotsman brandishing a knife and screaming every expletive in his wide vocabulary of Glaswegian death-threats. It would have been a familiar sound to any Roman guard on Hadrian's Wall. The man that was talking to me just a moment before then flung himself at the large Finn who was being assailed by his pursuer with a butter knife. I shot a glance at the elderly security guard, who stood wide-eyed and rooted to the spot. I piled in and dragged one Scotsman from the scrum whilst the Finn fought his way clear and ran away with blood streaming down his face. The Glaswegian then turned his ire on me just as two burly security guards arrived with sidearms. This seemed to calm the Scotsmen down but now, in a turn for the worse, I realised that the screaming was at me and it was coming from a large drunken woman who was berating me in Finnish; a language singularly equipped with rolled r's for the job of expressing hatred. She recognised me from my being on the stage earlier and assumed that the Glaswegians were with me and were musicians. My wife took on the Finn whilst a tall Norwegian explained to the guards that I had tried to stop the fight and that the two assailants were not part of the orchestra. The Scots were cuffed and led away. I was then astonished to be spat at by the woman who then incited the crowd to chant 'Foreign animals out', in Finnish. During this entire time, the elderly guard had not moved. He then apologised to my wife and I and suggested it would be better if we left the scene.

The next morning we were both summoned to the Captains' quarters. I dressed in blazer and tie as I had a feeling this was going to be a bit of a showdown and if I wasn't careful, I was going to get stitched up for something that was seriously not my fault. I was right. The Captain spoke English with a Finland-Swede accent and announced that when the ship docked at Stockholm, we were to leave the ship and return to England with the entire orchestra. I tried to explain to him that none of the combatants were musicians and that I had never seen the Glaswegians before. He shook his head saying that he had made up his mind and that he never changed his mind once it was made up.

At this point, my wife intervened in Swedish, to his astonishment, and did not draw breath for about two minutes other than to show him a hand-written note. The elderly guard was called into the room, looking sheepish. There was a pause. The Captain looked up. "Mr Dalby, it appears I have made a mistake and owe you an apology. I would be very pleased if you and your orchestra will remain on the ship to see out your contract and would be delighted if you and your wife would accept my apology by joining me at the Captain's table for dinner tonight." Susanne looked smug. The tall Norwegian had apparently written a note saying he had witnessed the whole thing and that not only was I not in any way to blame but that I had, in fact, acted to safeguard where the security guard present had failed spectacularly. The Captain had no option but to lose face and stand down. Phew!

We returned to England, utterly exhausted, and in a strange jetlag, as we had been playing till late and sleeping in during the day. Wide-eyed and awake I popped out to the 7-Eleven in Ealing at about 3:00 am and returned with some snacks to see the breaking news. On February 24th, 1991, the Coalition Forces, spearheaded by the Americans, crossed into Kuwait and headed toward Kuwait City. The Gulf War had begun in earnest.

Chapter 21
Back to the East

In the Spring of 1991, I began to have thoughts of recording another album. The ITV series of *Jeeves and Wooster* had just come onto our screens and I wrote a song with the opening scene in mind where Jeeves is sent by the agency in answer to Bertie Wooster's request for a valet. Unfortunately, it had been Boat Race Night and Bertie had been clinked for trying to steal a policeman's helmet but released in the morning, after coming up before the beak and fined five shillings and bound over to keep the peace. Jeeves enters the premises and fixes the very hungover Bertie with one of his 'pick me-ups' and, as soon as the explosion in his throat dies down and as soon as he is able to speak, Bertie engages Jeeves on the spot and the rest is the stuff of legend.

As I had played at the Oxford and Cambridge Boat Race Ball on a number of occasions, I knew the high jinks the young Oxbridge types get up to, so this rang true with me. One Ball wasn't even cancelled when the Poll Tax riots blocked the whole of central London. I managed to get across Trafalgar Square through tear gas, police horses and anarchists and arrived at the Savoy to find people arriving in full evening dress, late, but determined to carry on into the early hours. It was one such Sunday morning, when I myself was the victim of some over-indulgence, that a simple tune came into my head and I endeavoured to write some words:

Hair of the Dog

Tell the birds to keep it low, tell the sun he needn't show
Tell the dog that bit me, I'm going to bite him back
So mix your famous pick-me-up, that can start a three-ton truck
Danced all night with this girl
What was her name again, Mable or Pearl?
What a price I had to pay, it was worth it anyway
When I danced the Charleston upon a baby grand
Perhaps I'll think more clearly the next time
I Charleston over a Bechstein
So, to clear this mental fog, fix me a Hair of the Dog!
Now the pain I felt all night that my ears were on too tight
Has completely vanished like the pale moonlight
And now it's five o'clock in the morning, the sun's appeared without warning
and I feel like a Greek God
Thanks to that Hair of the Dog – Yeah!

I took it to Edward Kassner at President Records who sucked on his cigar looking doubtful but I knew he liked it.

"You vant me to publish this?" It's not as good as 'Crrrooner'!

"Well, it's different. Crooner was a swing song. This is bluesy. It's a hangover song. Anyway, I need a new album to give to Malaysia Air Services; they want to buy 500 copies for their clients as it's their 30th Anniversary."

There was a long silence.

"David! Ve need a new contract for der Gramophones!"

I had had an extraordinary double whammy of good luck. Firstly, my lawyer friend in Hong Kong, Ted Marr, had phoned to say he had persuaded Michel Galopin, the Banqueting Director of The Peninsula, to invite us out there, over the Christmas and New Year period for ten days. Secondly, I had a call from the Harrison and Parrott Agency to say that they needed to book a 1930s' orchestra for their client MAS to perform in Kuala Lumpur. The fee was generous.

The day before we were due to record vocals for the album (we had laid down the band tracks), I had agreed to play in a cricket match with 21 other like-minded musicians. It was a sweltering afternoon and I was in the field for some considerable time getting dehydrated. After the match, there was plenty of cold beer and a fabulous curry laid on by some marvellous Indian cricket and jazz fans. The following morning, I went into the studio and tried to sing the *Sheik of Araby*. The producer looked over his glasses and suggested I go away and warm up! When I recorded the 'Hair of the Dog', I really did mean it! The voice soon cleared up and the album was released under the title *Let's Do It Again*, which was a dreadful fifties pastiche but the label insisted on it. The song was published by guess who? Yup!…Edward Kassner!

We had a great summer with some lovely gigs and I made a very good friend from France, a dyed-in-the-wool Bonapartist called Thierry Lentz. He worked for a large national utility company named SAUR and was responsible for corporate events. One very special event was at a beautiful hotel in Annecy, not far from Geneva. The Imperial Palace was situated by a lake and we arrived in glorious sunshine. The hotel was an Art Deco dream and no sooner had we arrived, when we were invited to have lunch before being shown to our rooms. The sound-check lasted for an eternity as with all French sound engineers who have no idea how to balance a 1930s' band…mind you, there are plenty of rubbish ones in the UK too. We all appeared in (fairly) good order at the bar at around 8:30 dressed and ready to go. Thierry joined us and explained that the audience was made up of civic dignitaries from the town. Bankers, accountants, council officials, the mayor and such-like. He said there were no women and these were some of the grimmest, greyest men on the planet and that they would probably get up and leave once we started playing. He also said we must have what we liked at the bar as the tab was on him. So ill-advised! He also said that he had hired two comics, French funny men, to do a warm-up before we came on. The speeches after dinner droned on and on and on until finally, Thierry unleashed his funny men, to liven up the proceedings. These two guys had everything, they could mime like Marcel Marceau, they had Pierrot and Comedia dell'arte off to a tee and oh, how they worked. Not a ripple did they get in 45 minutes. I had never witnessed two funny men die like that since I was at Thomas Cooke's 150th Anniversary at Cliveden and sat on the other side of a revolving stage as Peter Skellern and Richard Stilgoe sweated through a 30-minute set with guest of honour Princess Diana and global clients who didn't understand a word.

Back in Annecy, at this point, Thierry popped his head around the curtain, where the band were seated and had been for an hour, and said, "Something very fast to open, please, in two minutes." I was trying to convey this to the band that we were now going to play *Is You Is or Is you Ain't* instead of the number they had in front of them. They all scrabbled through their pads to find the new number and at this moment up went the curtain, the microphones went live and the first thing the clients heard was me saying to the band, "Oh shit, I've blown it!"

The band eventually all got their music up but the saxophones had great difficulty playing, as their shoulders were going up and down with tears running down their cheeks, trying desperately to blow their instruments and suppress their laughter. The civic dignitaries couldn't wait to put on their 'Flasher's Macs' and make for the exit. When the last one had left, Thierry approached the stage, and I was about to apologise when he said, "tell your boys to wait there, please."

He left the room and came back with his beautiful assistant brandishing bottles of the finest Champagne shouting, "And now at last the party begins. As long as you keep playing, we keep bringing you the champagne." My wife and I left at 2:30 am with Tony, the Essex bass player, lying on his back with his bass on top of him but still continuing to play. Up in our fabulous Deco room, we ordered Steak Tatar and a glorious bottle of Burgundy to see off the night. At Geneva airport, the next day, various members of the band looked like extras in a Zombie film especially the saxes. We felt great!

The summer passed with some lovely events around the country until it was time to embark on our trip to Kuala Lumpur. I was quite delighted to receive the airline tickets from the Harrison and Parrott Agency and discovered they had booked both Susanne and I first-class tickets on what was a longish flight. We boarded at Gatwick and I apologised to the boys that they were flying economy but that's life! When we flew BA to Dubai, they all got upgraded. I loved the idea of having a glass of champagne in my hand before we had even taken off and, the darling stewardess kept bringing Satay chicken sticks, which were absolutely delicious with the Veuve Clicquot. By the time we had left UK airspace, I had eaten about nine of these Satays and was feeling comfortably replete. I was embarrassed to discover, when the stewardess came by again, that this was just an appetiser and the main meal was about to be served with a choice of poached salmon or filet steak! The rest of the flight escapes my memory but I suspect, I slept well until we touched down in Kuala Lumpur, having flown over my childhood paradise of Singapore. As the door opened, a smiling steward handed me a weighty carrier bag to add to my hand luggage and wished me well for the concert. We walked directly into the airport via a tube and so did not experience the shock of the heat outside until we left the airport to board the waiting bus. It was so hot and humid it took your breath away. We were grateful to get on the air-conditioned transport and at this point, my curiosity got the better of me and I opened the sealed carrier bag. It contained a number of goodies such as chocolates but included, I was incredulous to discover, a bottle of XO Rémy Martin and a bottle of vintage 'Grand Dame' Veuve Clicquot champagne. Wow! This was incredibly generous. We drove through the neon streets of KL and headed to the most prominent-looking hotel on the skyline, The Shangri-La or as Louis Armstrong once famously said, "Really La!" Waiting in the reception, the boys were all allocated their rooms on the 16th floor and I noticed that my wife and I were being kept for last. A charming and pretty Malaysian girl had been handing out the keys, once the band had registered but with us, she said, "I will show you to your room." We entered the lift and passed the 16th floor and just kept going until we reached the 24th floor when the doors opened to reveal that we had been allocated the Penthouse Suite. It had a stunning drawing room and two bathrooms with a panorama window that went all the way around. In the hallway to the suite, was a beautiful display of carnations with yet another bottle of champagne on ice! This was supposed to be work!

We played a two-hour set to around five hundred disinterested VIPs over a longish dinner and that was it. I have to ask the question though, why are very rich VIPs always disinterested? I think they are permanently bored and have little or no appreciation of fine arts and music unless they are buying a painting or objets d'arts as a financial investment. There are, of course, exceptions but on this evening, they were not invited. We played well enough and enjoyed the luxury and the fine weather for the rest of our stay. I was rather surprised when the representative arrived to pay me and handed me a large wallet of £50 notes, a lot of them. I dispensed these to an enthusiastic ensemble of musicians and with the remainder, decided that, as we had nothing to rush back for and that we would be returning to the East in December, a holiday in Malaya might be called for.

As a lad growing up in Singapore, my family had taken holiday-time far up the East coast of the Malayan Peninsula and, in particular, Kuala Terengganu, which I remembered for having long, beautiful, deserted golden beaches, fanned

Me working hard at the Shangri-La in Kuala Lumpur

by swaying palms and clear, warm water of the South China Sea. It was an area favoured by turtles for laying eggs as there were very few humans about. I was keen to revisit this paradise from my boyhood memories.

I booked into a motel sort of place by phone with the help of the concierge in the Shangri-La and booked us on a flight that took off around 3:00am from KL. We had to check out of the hotel at midday so we had plenty of time to amuse ourselves in the Karaoke bars of KL. These were mostly populated by Japanese tourists who take Karaoke very seriously and the worse the singer, the greater the respect for such bravery. I really enjoyed many memorable performances of songs like *Ebory an Ibolee* (Ebony and Ivory) and even, quite surprisingly, *Rocck Romond* (Loch Lomond) which was very popular among the Japanese who love anything Scottish, particularly Scotch whiskey, which they were consuming in impressive quantities.

Such hedonistic pursuits cannot go on forever and we left these songbirds to their art and taxied off to the airport to board a small aircraft which was full with around 50 passengers. The flight had been delayed by poor weather conditions and we took off just after 4:00 am. I was quite surprised that the passengers were all Malay, Indian and Chinese with no holidaymakers like us on board. It was pleasant then to hear the friendly voice of the Captain giving us our flight briefing in a broad Mid-Lothian accent. He did, however, warn us that, as the weather up the East Coast was subject to the monsoon, we could expect a bumpy ride, and we must keep our seatbelts fastened at all times. We had seen from our panorama window, from the top floor of the Shangri-la, what a spectacular full-blown electric storm could look like during the monsoon season. The lightning was awesome and terrifying at the same time. It was not the sort of thing you would choose to fly through but we had chosen to do precisely that. The flight resembled one of those switchback rides in an amusement park, where most of the participants get off looking green. Our small aircraft was battered and billowed as the Captain struggled to keep us above the clouds, which were being constantly lit up by the blue lightning. After nearly an hour of this, the dawn came up, and I was able to see that we were over the coast, through a small break in the clouds. The Captain had spotted this too and the plane went into a steep dive towards this hole. Coming out of this hole, we saw with horror that the sea wasn't very far below us and the pilot pulled us steeply out of the dive to straighten up. This was a passenger flight but felt more like being in a Stuka dive bomber. In the distance, a few miles off, the landing lights of the coastal airport came into view and we started the remainder of our descent, being rocked violently from side to side. I heard the landing gear go down and some people on the flight were sobbing. I clutched my drink firmly. Suddenly, just as we were about to touch down, a huge gust lifted the right-wing of the plane so violently that I, in a window seat behind the left-wing, saw with some consternation that the same left-wing was going to hit the runway if we continued on this course. Then the left wheel connected with the runway with such force that there was an almighty crack as the overhead lockers gave up the unequal fight and many flew open, with hand luggage crashing down on screaming passengers in the aisle seats. We were still on one wheel with the pilot in a death struggle with Nature to right the plane and keep the left-wing tip from hitting the runway. I had nearly spilt my gin and tonic during the impact, that's how bad it was, but as a seasoned flyer, I had caught it on its way back down and it remained in the glass. But the Captain was winning and soon the right wheel impacted on the ground and the aircraft was quickly stabilised and brought to a standstill, amidst the sobs and whimpers of many traumatised passengers, stumbling over the wreckage of spilled hand-luggage. The Captain came on the intercom to apologise and I led a round of applause for his skill and courage in setting us down safely.

We disembarked from the flying death trap and made our way to the hotel. Everything was damp and moist. It wasn't even very warm. Our lodging was a classic, Malay-style, chalet on stilts, right by the sea but a bit of a hike from the main hotel, where we would eat. It would have been a charming place but for the fact that it was cold and raining. My wife started to unpack a change of clothes when she suddenly let out a heartfelt, Swedish expletive and pointed at the verandah, "Oh! Herre God!" Squatting on the railing of the verandah appeared to be King Kong's baby brother. He wasn't small enough to be a monkey nor big enough to be an ape but, perhaps, a Bonobo of the ape family. What he was, though, was quite threatening. About three foot off the ground and with glowering eyes lacking in any respect whatsoever. I shouted through the glass door and gestured him to shoo! He did not appear to be even remotely impressed and the eyes glowered even more darkly. Well, I wasn't having this on my holiday. I grabbed a broom and slid open the glass door and made threatening gestures towards him with the brush end of the utensil. At this, he drew himself up to his full height to reveal a muscular chest, scarred from fighting. He then snarled such a snarl as to reveal two massive yellow incisors and a complete set of pointed canines that had the requisite effect of discouraging any aggressors, which I clearly was. At this stage in the battle, I felt it was a good time for a tactical withdrawal, to consolidate my position. I backed off slowly and slid the glass door shut. My wife had a bag of peanuts in her handbag, taken from the plane and she threw them at me. I opened the wrapper and then slid the door open, just enough for me to throw the bag onto the verandah floor. King Kong Jnr. dived and snatching the bag and swinging back onto the balcony and then up into a tree was with him, the work of a moment. Not one of my greatest victories but he was gone. My wife then said she was going to shower but I was to keep watch in case he decided to return with all his mates as in *Greystoke – The Legend of Tarzan*.

For a moment, there was peace but for the buzz of the jungle insects by the shore, and the crashing of the waves. This peace was shattered once more by a high-pitched scream from the bathroom. With an oath of "Dear God", I grabbed my broom and rushed into the bathroom where my wife was cowering in the corner of the shower closet, clutching a towel, and starring at a nameless horror on the opposite wall. Well, he wasn't the biggest I have ever seen, remembering the bird eating spider up a coconut tree in Singapore in the 60s, but he was certainly sporting an impressive leg-span of some five inches, with a stunning green and red abdomen and was enjoying his warm, damp corner and objected to intruders too big to eat. This time, however, my vorpal blade went snicker-snack and the defeated arachnid went galumphing back (The Jabberwocky). In normal English, that meant that I caught him a whack with the broom and he scuttled off via the glassless window of the shower compartment. With great reservation, my wife continued her shower, nervously as I kept guard outside with my trusty broom.

The next hour passed without any further ado and having calmed down, we dressed to go over for dinner in the hotel. We had been, or rather I had been, forced to the conclusion that Kuala Terengganu, during the monsoon, was not the place to be unless you were Johnny Weissmuller or similar. We then agreed that in the morning, we would check out and head off somewhere where the sun shone. I felt like the boy in the song *Hello Mudder, Hello Fader here I am in Camp Grenada*. We went into the long dining room which was sparsely populated with a few hotel guests, and the waiter showed us to a table by the far wall by another glassless window. What could possibly go wrong here? Drinks arrived and we were just starting to relax as the various courses of Malaysian cuisine were brought to the table. My wife had a large bowl of vegetables in front of her and was just helping herself to them, when King Kong Jnr.'s mate came powering through the window, onto our table and grabbed the whole bowl and skedaddled, to the howls of the pursuing waiters. We were moved to another table away from the window and drank until we found the whole episode amusing.

The next morning, I explained to the receptionist that we had decided to curtail our stay. She was very understanding but she said there was no transport out. All flights had been suspended and our aircraft had made it into the local press as a 'close call'! Trains were, likewise, suspended because of mudslides. She suggested she call a hotel in Penang, over on the far West side, to see how the weather was there. It turned out it was hot and sunny and they did have vacancies. "It's an 11-hour drive in a car and I can order you a taxi if you would like.?"

"A taxi?? What would that cost?"

She gave me the figure in dollars and when I converted it, we were only talking about £70 for him making a 22-hour round journey. This was incredible and we agreed immediately.

The journey, Northwest over the entire Malay peninsula, was a fascinating one and took in the fabulous scenery of the Cameron Highlands, named after the geologist William Cameron, who surveyed the area in 1885 for development. It is today a natural reserve for many species of flora and fauna, with three good roads connecting it. In 1992, there was just Route 59, a B road of red mud, with one restaurant along the way for a stopover to eat. After a seemingly endless drive of ten hours, we finally reached the crossing onto Penang Island, where our driver had called ahead and another taxi was waiting to take us onto the ferry.

We said farewell to our chap who, amazingly, turned on his taxi light 'for hire' in the hope of getting a return fare! After a short ferry trip, our new driver drove us up to the smart-looking hotel, and we checked in at nearly midnight. A quick nightcap was called for and we turned in to sleep the sleep of the dead.

I awoke in a cold, air-conditioned bedroom, darkened by blackouts, and with great trepidation, pulled them back, along with the balcony door, to be hit by a waft of glorious sunshine, a warming breeze and a vision of chaps going about in shorts and sunglasses. The next six days were to make up for all the trials and tribulations of the past 48 hours. The weather was wonderful, the hotel was very comfortable and the island of Penang was full of exotic things to see. We hired a jeep, with air-conditioning, and toured the island's treasures of temples, including the fabulous Buddhist monastery, the Kek Lok Si Temple, built high up into the rock-face slopes of Air Itam. The main attraction is the pagoda of Rama VI and a 100-foot tower. Climbing up in the heat, we stopped for a cold bottle of Tsing Tau. A Buddhist monk was nearby, selling trinkets and telling palms, and I decided to have mine read. It was all pretty good stuff and he rightly predicted that my fortune was in the East and if I moved West, my fortune would desert me. He then asked if we had children. When I replied in the negative, he produced a hideous wooden mask, brightly painted, with a large red tongue protruding from the leering open mouth. This unlikely incentive to procreation was, apparently, the God of Fertility, and if, as a woman, you touched the tongue before sleeping with your husband, it would aid in your being blessed with children. My wife couldn't imagine a scenario more ghastly and so, in a mood of pure mischief, I asked the monk how much for this icon. He laughed and said, "Whatever you wish to pay; it is for the monastery." I handed him a bundle of notes and we made our descent, with me clutching the mask, wrapped in newspaper. Complete and utter tosh, of course, but by March the following year, she had conceived and by late December 1992, our first daughter, Alexandra Charlotte, was born; a bouncing 9lbs of blue-eyed trouble.

The remainder of the stay I can only describe as pure heaven. The hotel had a large buffet restaurant where the German, English and Russian tourists congregated, as they were on all-inclusive package deals with their tour operators. I had noticed that there was a gourmet restaurant to which fantastic reviews in the brochure had been written. Having arrived at the Buffet restaurant and observing hugely fat tourists pile unfeasible mountains of food onto their plates, I suggested that we might try the five-star restaurant which had a French name, long forgotten. Opening the door, we were greeted by an elegant man with a genuine French accent, in immaculate evening dress and in a nano-second, we were transported from an eat-all-you-can-carry trough to a smart one-Michelin Star restaurant. The candles were lit, the glasses sparkled, the decor was French 3rd Empire and there was a young cocktail pianist tinkling musically through some Debussy. A cold splash of 'reality water' seemed to hit me in the face as I was suddenly acutely aware that I was dressed similarly to the tourists next door; shorts, sandals, loud shirt. I quickly got a grip and asked if we might book a table for 8:00pm. The Maitre D' surmised my embarrassment and, keen not to lose a client in an empty restaurant, said, "M'sieur, it is fine, we are out of season and we do not enforce the dress code, please take a seat if you wish."

"Thank you but no, we will return in 30 minutes."

"Bien M'sieur."

30 minutes later, we re-appeared with my wife, in a long, figure-hugging gown of emerald green and self, in my working clothes of white dinner jacket and bow-tie. There were shouts of "Achtung! James Bond!" from the laughing German tourists and then the door swung open to admit us into the deep red plush of our own little 'La Gavroche' in Malaya, without the Roux brothers. As the only guests, we were greeted with champagne and some lovely amuse-bouche, whilst we perused the menu, before picking out the Lobster Thermidor and promising to return the following day for the Chateaubriand. Apart from the wine, everything was so inexpensive and the quality to die for. The staff appreciated us giving them something to do; the sommelier, the chef, the sous-chef, the pastry chef and especially the pianist, who enjoyed rising to the challenge of my requests. I think we ate there every night before we left and only twice did another couple come in, dressed, of course, in regulation flip-flops and loud shirt. The day and evenings passed quickly, as they always do when you are having such a wonderful time but we had to return to England, if only briefly.

We flew off to Hong Kong just before Christmas but after the ordeal at Terengganu airport, the landing at Kai Tak seemed almost peaceful. We were met at the airport by a driver in a smart, Bentley-Green hotel uniform with a cap, and taken by minibus to the impressive colonial facade of the Peninsula Hotel with its fleet of green Bentley motorcars, gleaming outside.

The Peninsula deserves a little mention. Opened in December 1928, the Peninsula is situated in the shopping precinct of Tsim Sha Tsui, on the mainland of Kowloon, and not far from the drop-off point of Star Ferry. It was designed in the colonial style and was supposed to be the 'finest hotel East of Suez', outshining even the Raffles Hotel in Singapore. It hosted Sunday concerts, and dances every night, as well as tea dances in the afternoon. Like the Raffles in the 30s, it became a favourite resort of celebrities such as Noël Coward and Charlie Chaplin. Clark Gable introduced the bartender, Jonny Chan, to the cocktail known as 'a screwdriver' after the confused barman had sent for the house electrician, who arrived with a selection. Jonny Chan was informed by the other guests that the drink was for none other than the star of *Gone with the Wind* and the story made the South China Morning Post. Within a short time, 'A Screwdriver' had overtaken the 'Gin and Tonic' as the most popular drink to be had at cocktail hour. Christmas Day, 1941 was an inglorious scene for the hotel as the venue where the Governor, Sir Mark Young and General CM Maltby surrendered to the Japanese commander. The hotel was renamed Toa Hotel (East Asia Hotel) and became the resort of high-ranking Japanese officers until the Japanese surrender on August 30th, 1945, which was formally accepted on September 15th at Government House. The name 'Peninsula' was restored.

And so it was that my orchestra, with an additional violinist called Wilf, became the resident band at one of the most famous hotels in the world. Ted Marr, the lawyer and Michel Galopin, the banqueting director, who had organised the trip, were there to greet us into the magnificent baroque-style Lobby, which is where we would be performing each evening. Although we were housed in the Kowloon Hotel close by, rather than the HK$1,000 a night Peninsular, we took all our meals in the Lobby and enjoyed the splendour and the cuisine of this marvellous place. All food was included but not drinks, except beer, which was free, big mistake! We performed each night for dancing and the wealthy Chinese and ex-patriots flocked to come and hear us. We finished usually around 11:00 pm and the band would head off to local bars especially Ned Kelly's in Tsim Sha Tsui, an Australian bar that hosted its own sit-in and blow big band. Amazingly, despite having to play for most of the evening, quite a few of the chaps did 'sit in' and have a blow with this band into the early hours. Christmas Eve was quiet in the hotel and I remember finishing early with a very wistful rendering of Silent Night, to which guests all applauded appreciatively, and Michel Galopin had his waiters bring several silver trays up to the stage glinting with glasses of chilled champagne. It was a lovely evening; Nice work if you can get it!

The Peninsula Hotel - Hong Kong

Christmas Day lunch was spent with the band as the only people in the Lobby and we exchanged small presents. The boys, usually so boisterous and rowdy, confessed to being a little home-sick at this time and missed being with their families. We had the whole day off and Boxing Day too but in the evening the hotel had planned a treat for us. A coach had been booked to take us to a boat and thence to Peng Chau, a small island just off Lantau, and known for its temples, fishing industry and seafood. Monsieur Galopin and his tall lady assistant, Siân from Wales, and two Chinese members of the hotel's publicity department were hosts along with a Chinese butler, looking for all the world like Odd Job from 007, in a bowler hat, tailcoat and spongebag trousers. We, the band, were the guests. We arrived at a bustling seafood market, in the dark, with lightbulbs randomly strung along a wet passageway full of oriental smells and shouts from the vendors. On either side were hundreds of buckets of water containing every specimen of edible seafood you could imagine. Our butler led the way, shouting orders to the vendors, squatting by their wares and bundles of dollar bills changed hands. He did not take any of these fish himself as they were to be delivered. Instead, he carried a large cool-box that we discovered contained many bottles of chilled Chablis. We arrived at a garishly lit restaurant and were seated at large round tables and immediately the delicious wine was passed around. In the centre of the table was a circular, revolving tray, and on this was a very large bowl, into which was tipped a huge quantity of long, grey-brown prawns, very much alive and producing a mass of writhing legs, heads and antennae. This was about the most unappetising spectacle you could imagine and I asked one of the Chinese staff chaps next to me if we were expected to eat live prawns. He said it was a speciality and gave me the Cantonese name which I didn't quite understand. He translated for me: "Drunken Prawns!" and added, "very good to eat". I looked around at the horror-stricken faces of the musicians. Just then, the butler emptied the contents of a bottle of rice wine into the writhing bowl and I noticed a slight slowing down of movement. Then a whole bottle of Rémy Martin Cognac followed it and I quickly learnt the Chinese way of making a prawn say "Woof!" You throw in a lighted match! The poor creatures quickly turned a pretty pink and all movement stopped. I thought Dave, the guitarist, was going to faint. Even Tony, the Essex bass player was lost for an expletive and the only sound was a faint whistling as the air was expelled from the shells. The prawns were served up, piping hot, and as fresh as anything can be, that had been alive, just 60 seconds earlier. I have to confess I have rarely, if ever, tasted anything so delicious, even if the cooking method bordered on the barbaric. A lot of wine was consumed at that moment as people got over the shock and the band soon recovered their boisterous spirits. It was not something you would forget easily though.

Our final performance was on New Year's Eve, to see in 1992, which was a belter of a party with the guests in masks and fantastic costumes. The following morning Ted Marr invited Susanne and I to join him for hair of the dog 'Snowballs' at the Mandarin Hotel on Hong Kong Island. We took the Star Ferry over to Jung Wan (Central) and the stiff breeze, blowing off the water through the open-sided boat, certainly blew away the cobwebs from the night before. A short taxi ride and we arrived at the Mandarin where the morning party was well underway. Ted was there to meet us in one of his very loud trademark jackets. He had briefed me that it was a dressy event and no one would get in without a jacket and tie so I was fully blazered-up with Susanne in a posh frock. We were served 'Snowballs'; a bright yellow, frothy cocktail of Advocaat, Vodka and Champagne, and the effect was pretty instantaneous. Soon we joined the throng of laughing gweilohs, shouting at the tops of our voices in an attempt to get, whatever fatuous conversation we had said. Ted beamed and of course, knew everybody whom he addressed regardless of gender as 'daarling' in that gentle Australian accent, that he always made sound so sophisticated. Given that he had been partying 'til around 4:00 am at the Pen, he looked amazing. But that was Ted, the organiser of the global party and events company, known as the South China Coast Ball. Ted had taken his guests from Macau to Cuba and St Petersburg and as such, was practically bulletproof where hangovers were concerned. Just then about 40 army musicians materialised on the staircase leading down to the lobby where we were. They were all in number one dress uniform, from the Anglian Regiment, who were stationed in Hong Kong at the time. Two burly sergeants presented a brace of gleaming Post horns to scream out the high-pitched calls antiphonally to each other before embarking on the rousing 'Post horn Gallop', the band accompanying with a feisty rendition of *D'ye Ken John Peel* played faster and more accurately than I had ever heard it. It was sensational. Every New Year's Day thereafter, I have endeavoured to open the batting with a 'Snowball' or two to clear the mental fog. The lunch was passed over as we had been so well looked after with canapés and champagne and it was just left to grab an afternoon siesta before rejoining the boys for a last night on the town over in Tsim Sha Tsui. The following morning Ted came over from Hong Kong to see us off and presented us with a lovely book on Hong Kong's history, just published, and Michel Galopin presented me with a silver letter-opener inscribed 'The Peninsula'. We said our goodbyes and headed toward Kai Tak airport for the long 'red-eye' flight home to see what 1992 had in store for us.

Chapter 22
Annus Horribilis

1992 was a year of considerable ups and downs in England for the economy, the government and perhaps, most famously, as the title of this chapter attests, for the Royal Family. The Conservatives won a fourth term general election in April, with John Major as Prime Minister. The Sun newspaper claimed the victory with its iconic headline: "It's The Sun wot won it!" to describe its election-day front page, ridiculing the Welsh Labour leader Neil Kinnock, who resigned a few days later. He then joined the Euro gravy train as MEP, where he remained until 2004 as Vice-President of the European Commission. The Conservatives presided over a disastrous year including 'Black Wednesday' (September 16th), in which the government suspended the UK's membership of the European Exchange Rate Mechanism, and unemployment soared to a five-year high as the pound plummeted and the UK sank into recession. The Heritage Minister, David Mellor resigned after press speculation that he had been having an affair with the actress, Antonia de Sancha, and was replaced by Iain Sproat, about whom more will be said shortly.

For the Queen and the Royal Family, it could hardly have been worse. It was the Queen's Ruby Jubilee but in March, the Palace was forced to announce that the Duke and Duchess of York were to separate after just six years of marriage during which two British newspapers wrote that Sarah 'Fergie' had not conducted herself in a manner fitting her title on a trip to California. In August, the Daily Mirror published excruciatingly embarrassing photos of Sarah and Texas businessman, John Bryan, in the infamous toe-scandal. The Queen issued a statement that she would not be responsible for Sarah's considerable debts. In April, Princess Anne had announced her divorce from Captain Mark Phillips, after 18 years of marriage. In June, a biographer, Andrew Morton, had published a controversial book *Diana: Her True Story*, revealing that Princess Diana had made five suicide attempts on discovering Prince Charles had resumed his affair with his previous girlfriend, Mrs Parker Bowles, shortly after the birth of Prince William in 1982. In November, Windsor Castle was badly damaged by fire, with the cost of repairs being some £36.5 million. The Queen agreed to start paying tax and opened Buckingham Palace to tourists to help pay the restoration costs. Very few works of art were damaged but the largest of the State Apartments, St George's Hall, the Crimson Drawing Room and the Green Drawing Room were completely gutted. In December, Charles, Prince of Wales and Princess Diana announced their separation. Finally, to end a truly horrible year for Her Majesty, The Sun newspaper leaked the Queen's Christmas Message on December 23rd.

Against this backdrop of political and Royal turbulence, my life took on some new responsibilities. Following the happy jaunts to the East, there weren't so many bookings for the band in the Winter and Spring of 1992 and I kept going via my other singing ventures with various vocal groups. These included 'The Nigel Brookes Singers', 'The John McCarthy singers' and the 'Ambrosian Opera Chorus'. The BBC had a live, weekly radio show called *Friday Night is Music Night* and on so many occasions, I turned up to these in one choir or other; sometimes as a soloist and sometimes fronting my own band, 'The Grahamophones' who the audience, being of a certain age, loved. The members of the BBC Concert Orchestra got to know my face pretty well but, on one occasion, we took them all by surprise. They had no idea that Martin Loveday, the outstanding leader of the BBC Concert Orchestra, had played on a few of our albums and had even performed with us for an outside broadcast in Worthing. We played our allocated three numbers and then, for the last one, we played *Is You Is Or Is You Ain't My Baby*, at a crackling speed, and the orchestra were astonished to notice Martin get up from his leader's desk and rush around behind the orchestra to the podium where we were performing. As I completed my vocal, he ripped off a jazz solo in the style of Stephane Grappelli with such brilliance that you could hear the intake of breath from the live audience and the Concert Orchestra. The roar of appreciation that followed is perhaps the loudest I have ever heard on that programme, which went out live across the land on that Friday evening.

Spring arrived and my wife had some rather special news for me. I don't know about the fertility mask from Penang but she was expecting a very unplanned baby. The problem was that we lived in a very nice Art Deco flat in Ealing with one bedroom and a smaller room which served as an office and home to a small parrot named Minnie 'The Moocher'. This certainly wouldn't do to bring a new arrival into the world, so I began to make inquiries into getting a mortgage to buy a place of our own. It quickly became clear that none of the building societies were interested in lending money to first time buyers in these very troubled financial times. Either they required a huge deposit or they just shook their heads at the idea of my being a self-employed musician and my wife a self-employed translator. A friend of mine in the City said the banks were even harder to get mortgages from. Enter Mr Pinney…

Claude Pinney was a sort of cross between a bank manager and a fairy godfather. In 1985, shortly after I had left Trinity, I set up my 1930s' band. Pickings were fairly slim to start with and I still had a debt on my Barclaycard. I was in the middle of filming a documentary with the BBC, which was an astonishing piece of free publicity. Shortly after the programme went out on BBC 2, at peak viewing on a Friday, I had a call from my bank in Haslemere asking me to come down to speak to them. I went down, confident that, with this film behind me, they would be happy to support me in my career. I emerged from my bank manager's office with my heart in my mouth at the realisation that they had in effect foreclosed on me by demanding back, in full, the debt on my card by the end of the month. I was in trouble. I returned to London and the following morning a stack of letters arrived. They had been forwarded by the BBC and were all from viewers to me saying what a marvellous programme it had been and where could they come and hear the band. One was from 'Tiny' Winters, bassist to Ambrose and his Orchestra, another was from the widow of the great bandleader, Lew Stone, inviting me to tea in Richmond, and another was from the actor Derek Nimmo. At last, came a typed letter on headed paper which said, something along the lines of, how much he had enjoyed the programme as he was a great fan of the '30s' British Dance Bands and (crucially), that he was the manager of the Wimbledon branch of the National Westminster Bank and if ever I should need a friendly bank manager, I was to call him on this number to arrange to meet for lunch. *Thank you, God*! I wasted no time in having lunch with Mr Pinney who basically, took over my debt from Haslemere and increased my credit. The Barclays manager was furious! He said it was very unprofessional of Mr Pinney to tout for business from one of their clients. It transpired that I wasn't the only band he had pulled the plug on. This same manager had foreclosed on a loan to a rock band run by four lads from Charterhouse for a debt of around £9,000. The band went on to be quite famous, they were called *Genesis!*

And so it was, in 1992, when the phone rang, it was Mr Pinney, Bank Manager, asking me again to join him for lunch. I had things on my mind. He asked how it was all going and if I had any more Royal engagements on the horizon but my thoughts were about house-buying and I mentioned that no building society would consider giving me a mortgage to buy a flat as I was self-employed and that there was a new arrival on the way. He looked at me with wide-eyed disbelief. "Why didn't you come to me?"

By the time we had finished the bottle of excruciating English wine, I was practically on the housing ladder. I wanted to get back to South London where the properties in some areas were still cheap but would soon be going up significantly, as the Yuppies spilled over from Fulham and Clapham. We managed to find a flat in Earlsfield, just South of Wandsworth Bridge. It was a hot tip from the estate agent that the area was the next expected to a see sharp rise in property value. The flat was an upstairs of a terrace of apartments that had an A and B flat to each building. The decor was hideous, there was no central heating but there was a loft conversion, with no planning permission, so it was in effect, a three-bedroom flat at a snip. Claude Pinney was delighted and rubber-stamped the mortgage to the wide-eyed astonishment of a young Indian lady from NatWest Home Loans. By July, we were in and busy stripping and painting and restoring the fireplace and prepping up the nursery for the December arrival. The area was brilliantly served with pubs and restaurants and a railway station straight into Clapham Junction and then to central London or the City.

Work, despite the depression, was quite encouraging, and I had spent a considerable amount of time writing a theatre show entitled *What ho! Wodehouse.* The first half used short clips from various novels, interspersed with music from the on-stage band. An actor from Dulwich played Pelham Grenville Wodehouse, John Touhey from the BBC narrated the storyline and Jeremy de Satgé, from Trinity, and myself played various parts, including Bertie Wooster and Jeeves, Aunt Agatha and assorted characters, Bingo Little, Tuppy Threepwood etc. The second half concerned Wodehouse and his internment in occupied Europe and his subsequent broadcasts from the Adlon Hotel in Berlin, based on a book by Rt. Hon. Iain Sproat called *Wodehouse at War.* I took the script to the BBC and they loved it. I also contacted Iain Sproat, who was delighted when I asked if he would like to come into a BBC studio to be interviewed about his book. He invited me to the House of Commons on a delicious Summer's evening to drink gin and tonics on the balcony overlooking the Thames at a table next to the former Labour Leader, Neil Kinnock, who had so recently suffered such a humiliating defeat. Sproat and I were kindred spirits with our great passions being cricket and the life and works of PG Wodehouse. We both agreed that we had to clear Wodehouse's name, in the eyes of the public, as most people in the UK and the USA had been weaned on the myth that Wodehouse was a collaborator.

That Summer also produced another invitation from Thierry Lentz to perform in La Rochelle for a large corporate party. This was a great success and the crowd were mostly younger people who found they could dance 'Ceroc' steps to our music; a kind of French Lindy Hop that was very popular in France at that time. The next day, Thierry invited us all to a fabulous seafood restaurant on the seafront and he listened agog as we regaled him of the oft-told story of the Chinese drunken prawns. On the journey back to the airport, Thierry said it would be very nice if we could do another CD but one which included the popular Charles Trenet song *La Mer*. It must have been the sea air as when I said Kassner/President would not put up the money so soon after the last one, Thierry shrugged a Gallic shrug and said, "Ow, much do you need?"

And so it was that I found myself back in Leicester Square in the office of Edward Kassner, me sat on a low chair looking up at his doubtful expression and him puffing his cigar from a much higher chair. I explained to him that we had a sponsor, SAUR, a French utilities company and that we had been working for them in Le Touquet, Annecy and La Rochelle.

"And how much can ve expect from zis Frrrrench shponsor?" asked Edward, still frowning.

I told him…

"David!! Ve need a new contract for zer Gramophones!"

It was amazing that I could now combine the music for the new album with the music I needed for the *What ho! Wodehouse!* show and I spent much of the Autumn planning and revising the script and sorting out arrangements for the album. Clive Dunstall, our hugely talented pianist, rose to the challenge of composing a new arrangement of the Charles Trenet song, *La Mer*, keeping it

Our 4th Album with President Records

very much in the style of that lazy, lilting French crooner. The brilliant film composer, Ann Dudley, kindly sent me her score of *Jeeves & Wooster*, the title music from the new Tiger Aspect television series featuring Steven Fry and Hugh Laurie. Incredibly, she said we could re-arrange it as we pleased, whilst not changing the melody, and of course, she would get all the publishing royalties. I put it in the safe hands of the Scottish arranger, Colin Skinner, who worked it for saxophone solo instead of violin, and it worked very well. I had the idea of theming the album like a 1930s' luxury liner, with the music from New York, London, Paris and Berlin. The cover featured a famous poster by the French artist, Cassandre, of the bow of the great liner; the S.S. Normandie called 'Transatlantique'.

December arrived but no sign of the expected little one as yet. Eventually, on 22nd December, the doctors announced that my wife be taken into St George's Hospital, Tooting and induced. Finally, at around 6:00 pm on 23rd December, with my wife not at all amused that I was playing *For unto us a child is born* loudly on the CD player, in the delivery room, as she was being told not to swear by an old-school Jamaican mid-wife, a substantial pink bundle weighing in at nine and a half pounds was brought into the world, with an expression on her face of one who had been quite happy where she was and who pray, was responsible for this liberty? When I was assured that all my fingers were not, in fact, broken, and blood once more flowed through my right hand, I was handed the baby and marvelled at the great miracle of life that had brought Alexandra Charlotte Dalby into the world, eventually.

1993 opened with a flurry of activity for me as I began plans for a tour of the show *What Ho Wodehouse!* and prepared to get the music together for the new album. The BBC came up trumps by inviting me to take over Sheridan Morely's innovative *The Arts Programme*; a two-hour BBC Radio 2 spectacular, which went out on a Sunday night. Morely himself needed to fly to America in order to try and salvage his 1992 show *Spread a Little Happiness*; a biopic of Vivien Ellis. The Americans didn't buy it but this left his BBC producers struggling to fill a two-hour slot on a Sunday evening and so were delighted when my script arrived. Myself, John Touhey and Jeremy de Satgé all traipsed along to Broadcasting House and recorded the short clips from various hilarious Wodehouse novels with John narrating. I provided the linking music from my own band recordings of the Grahamophones and from original 78s, which I mastered onto digital minidisc for the BBC's tecky boys to edit together. On a separate day, Iain Sproat came into Broadcasting House and I did my first ever interview from the other side of the desk. Sproat was fantastic, as he was responsible for getting Prime Minister Harold Wilson to grant Wodehouse his knighthood, just before his death in February 1975. Between us, we opened up the story of the great injustice that had been meted out to Britain's finest ever writer of humorous novels. We had the whole two-hour show in the can inside a week and the BBC was delighted. It went out on Sunday, 28th March, 1993, between 8:00 and 10:00 pm, when a large number of people were returning home from the weekend break and had Radio 2 tuned in their cars. One such person was the jolly personage of theatre impresario, Dudley Russell, the Cotswolds-based husband of the poet of Pam Ayres.

It all started off very well, with Dudley organising a twenty-date theatre tour right across the country. Before we started, however, a letter arrived, framed in quite threatening language, saying that the BBC should not have gone ahead with the broadcast and, under no circumstances, must we attempt to perform this programme live, on pain of immediate recourse to stringent legal action for breaching copyright. It was signed by some lawyer who claimed to be acting for the Wodehouse family and the Wodehouse Trust. Since Wodehouse had died childless (his stepdaughter, Leonora Cazalet had died in 1944 and his wife Ethel had died in 1985), I wondered which family he could have meant. The last and youngest of his three brothers had died in 1951, so they had gone. In 1995, I befriended Rosie Wodehouse, whose father was an army officer and a cousin of PG Wodehouse but certainly no beneficiary. The Estate must have been huge and now, even greater with all the TV coverage and huge resurgence of popularity, especially in India and the USA. I took the trouble to phone up the legal firm and was surprised to find that the voice on the other end was open to negotiations. The tour still might go ahead. Several days later, a letter arrived but the terms of them granting us permission were, frankly, ridiculous and meant that practically all the profits of a three quarters full house would go to the Trust (or the lawyers). I took my own legal advice from a reputable partnership in Holborn. There was no doubt, the lawyer said, having read the script, that you are using less than one percent of any given book and as you are quoting the author, not plagiarising or in any way using a copyrighted work to sell your performance, you cannot be in breach of copyright. I put this to the Wodehouse Trust lawyer who became extremely aggressive and threatening saying that, whatever the cost, they would take legal action if any concerts went ahead and continue until we had run out of money. More than three-quarters of the programme was music from the band, quotes from his biographies and transcripts from his Berlin wartime broadcasts. I felt safe to continue. The tour was not a huge financial success as apart from the orchestra, we had a lady vocalist to sing *Bill* from *Showboat* (Jerome Kern/PG Wodehouse) and *Nice Work* from *Gay Divorce* by Gershwin (book by PGW), a narrator, an actor playing Plum himself and another actor playing Jeeves and Aunt Agatha and anyone else except Bertie Wooster (me). Dudley Russell, with admirable enthusiasm, booked some of the largest concert halls in England, including the Symphony Hall in Birmingham and the De Montford Hall in Leicester. We were about to perform at The Queen Elizabeth Hall in London when Dudley made an understandable mistake…

A photographer from the Daily Telegraph showed up at my flat in London to take a shot of me, in evening dress, glass of whisky beside me, reading *Wodehouse at War* by Iain Sproat. They wanted to write an article on the Wodehouse Berlin broadcasts and mention our tour. A few days later the phone rang and I recognised at once the shrill, metallic voice of a lawyer, incandescent with rage. I told him that my lawyers begged to differ and may have wound him up a little by signing off with a "Tinkerty-Tonk!" à la Bertie Wooster. We performed to a good-ish house in a Southend-on-Sea theatre but during the interval, Dudley phoned me and asked me to instruct the band and actors that there would be just one more performance before the tour was pulled. It appeared that the threats made against him by the Wodehouse Trust were just too real for him to risk and, as the show was only just above breaking even, he announced that the Wyvern Theatre in Swindon would be our last performance. Happily, the theatre was well-attended, and even Dudley deigned to make an appearance. He thought the show very good but needed some tweaking. Had he seen the show at the opening, we could have done that! We all had a bit of a drink in the bar and Titanic-like toasted the sinking ship that was What ho! Wodehouse.

Me, reading a copy of Wodehouse at War by Iain Sproat

As a postscript to the above, I have researched the Wodehouse Estate and it transpires that, while Plum had no children, he had married a widow named Ethel May, who had a daughter named Leonora. Plum loved her like a father and adopted her to become Leonora Wodehouse. In 1935, she married the charismatic Peter Cazalet. An Oxford cricketing blue, he played for Kent and the MCC. He was a Major in the Guards Armoured Division and went on to become the Queen's (later Queen Mother's) horserace trainer until his death in 1973. In 1944, Leonora was desperately fighting Plum's corner against the appalling accusations being made in the British press about his broadcasts from Berlin. She died suddenly after a minor operation. Plum said of her when he heard: "I had thought she was immortal." But she had had a child named Edward, born in 1936, who went on to become Sir Edward Cazalet, High Court Judge and principal trustee of the Wodehouse Estate. He was not at the Queen Mother's 100th birthday event at Windsor but his father's second wife is on the guest list as Mrs Peter Cazalet, so at least she heard our music, although blissfully unaware of the

149

work I had done to help clear the name of Leonora Cazalet's adopted father, PG Wodehouse!

Chapter 23
À l'Opéra de Lyon

The collapse of the tour had left a big hole in my finances and the work I had in with the Ambrosian Singers was not enough to support me through the Winter with a recession on. I heard word that an English chorus master, named Richard Cooke, had been appointed to Opera de Lyon in 1993, and that John Elliot-Gardiner had left to be replaced by the benign but disciplined Kent Nagano. Even better, he was looking for a high-baritone who had a decent knowledge of French with good pronunciation. I applied and drove down to a smart country house with my old Trinity pal and accompanist, Paul Chilvers, armed with an aria from an opera by Massenet, *Vision Fugitve*, featuring the debauched Herod, letching after his stepdaughter Salomé. We had performed it in concerts before and it went off to the approval of Lyon Opera's new chorus master. Being himself, a St Paul's chorister and a King's choral scholar, I wasn't surprised when a tricky, sight-reading test was brought out. It was a particularly meandering, modal phrase from 'Dona Nobis Pacem' by Vaughan Williams which was written for baritone solo. The chances of me not knowing it given my background were slim but Cookie, as we came to know him, had been auditioning opera singers who are quite famed for their poor standard of sight-reading. I had to sing it unaccompanied and I sang it perfectly but for an F# rising in the scale which fitted, and which I knew was wrong. "Almost perfect," he said, "can you try it once again and correct your one mistake?"

This time I sang the uncomfortable F natural in the rising scale and his face lit up with delight.

"Have you sung this before?" I shook my head.

"Had you sung that before?" asked Paul, suspiciously, as we walked back to the car.

151

"Of course not," I grinned and somehow, inexplicably, my pants did not catch on fire.

I arrived back in Earlsfield with baby Alex sitting on the floor and crawling at everything. Susanne, frazzled after a day with a ten-month-old baby that is desperate to walk, was not impressed. "If you think you are swanning off to France and leaving me to sort Christmas alone with Alex, you can think again!"

And so it was that I found myself booked on a flight to Lyon, with a wife and young baby. I had booked a comfortable apartment near the centre of town, just a short walk from the opera house itself. The opera was Don Giovanni, so there wasn't much for the chorus to sing but I was impressed by the standard of this young very international group. Several of the English singers had just come from Glyndebourne and others I knew from the Ambrosian Singers. Two Scottish singers, David and Valerie Stephenson, had brought a baby of a similar age to Alex, so it was good to have people to compare baby notes with.

Opéra Nationale de Lyon was a fabulous, neo-classical building, dating from 1830 and boasted first performances of operas such as Andrea Chénier in the 1880s. Back in September 1983, I had sung as a soloist in this magnificent building for a Radio France Musique broadcast with the Orchèstre de Lyon, under the baton of Serge Baudot, for the Berlioz Festival with the Pro Musica Chorus of London. There is a little anecdote worth telling…the chorus master was John McCarthy, of Ambrosian Singers fame and although it was an amateur chorus, a number of students were recruited from the Academy, Trinity and Guildhall. There was a little carrot on offer. As well as singing the great *La Damnation de Faust* by Berlioz, in the huge sports arena, there were soprano, baritone and bass solos up for grabs in another concert in the old Opéra de Lyon. John McCarthy had supplied the music for the 'traité d'orchestration' (a lecture-recital written by Berlioz in which he examines the development of orchestration from Gluck to Wagner) to a number of us students saying, the conductor would hear them sing and decide which solos would be sung by whom. The audition would be in France when we got there. I was one of those singers proposed by John McCarthy and duly turned up to sing my Gluck aria on a warm September afternoon in Lyon. I was amazed at how many sopranos were waiting in the hall outside the studio. Several tenors even said they were going for the baritone part, which I thought a bit thick! Two basses were immediately disappointed when it was announced that the bass soloist from Paris Opera, Jean-Marie Frémaux, was going to sing the bass solos. There then followed a rapid procession of sopranos from the Royal College, the Royal Academy and Guildhall, who had no sooner gone in to audition when the door opened and out they came, usually with the expression: "he's only hearing a few bars!" Finally, it was my turn and I went in clutching my score of Ephigénie en Aulide by Gluck. I sang the opening passage and glanced at Serge Baudot, who was watching me intently. I was waiting for him to say: "Merci, c'est assez"…but he didn't and I continued to the end of the short aria. He nodded and the receptionist smiled and opened the door of the studio where I joined the waiting throng of hopefuls. After a moment, the secretary emerged again with an awkward smile and said that the Maestro conveyed his thanks, and that they could all go now. There was an audible gasp of indignation and disbelief that was interrupted by a shout from inside the studio:

"Sauf le jeune baryton, je garderai le jeune baryton."

I walked up the corridor, with the other singers venting their vexation simultaneously when I heard John McCarthy call my name: "Where are you going, Graham? You're 'Le Jeune Baryton'! The Maestro wants to see you now to discuss the concert." I glanced back at the throng of sopranos and thought 'if looks could kill!'.

I rejoined my Trinity colleagues in the hotel, who had already heard the news and there my friends, who included Andy Busher, Louise Hemmings, Judith Bates and others, had a beer to celebrate that, where singers from the College and the Academy had failed, a Trinity man had prevailed. The concert went ahead in the beautiful ornate opera house with a soprano flown down from Paris Opera but who had a somewhat pronounced lisp. One of the main arias she had to sing was a huge blockbuster that was one of Maria Callas' party pieces *Divinité du Styx*. When she started singing during the run-through, there was an audible snort from the sopranos in the chorus behind me, as the repeated phrase Divinité du thteeexth just got funnier and funnier with each repetition. I sucked in my cheeks, to prevent myself laughing and tried not to notice that Jean Marie Frémaux, sitting next to me, was also struggling. The rest of the concert went off well but the newspapers, the next day gave the English sopranos the revenge they so badly desired:

*"Une lecture vivante, un orchestre de Lyon des bons soirs bien dirigé par Serge Baudo, Le Choeur 'Pro Musica' aussi bon que dans 'La Damnation de Faust', de belles voix de solistes, J.M. Frémaux et **Graham Dalby**; mais aussi*

malheureusement, une soprane dont nous ignorons le nom qui gagne à être oubliée..."

Translate: A lively lecture, 'The Orchestra of Lyon' in good form, well-directed by Serge Baudo, the Choir 'Pro Musica' just as good as in 'Damnation of Faust', the beautiful voices of soloists, J.M. Frémaux and Graham Dalby but also, unfortunately, a soprano whose name we do not know but would be better off forgotten...Ouch!

Back to 1993, I walked into that same Opera House in September, shortly after it had been inaugurated in May that year, following an astonishing architectural make-over by the controversial Jean Nouvel. From outside, the 1830s' shell of the opera house seemed untouched, with the vast statues of the Muses looking benignly down at aesthetes and music-lovers entering the portals of this temple of culture. The rehearsal studios were all brand-spanking new underground rooms with plenty of space for sound and good acoustics provided by glass walls and wood-panelled floors. During the break, I decided I would go upstairs to re-acquaint myself with this beautiful old building where I had sung a decade earlier. Nothing could have prepared me for the shock that awaited me. The lift opened to reveal long corridors of blood-red silk and gleaming chrome. I followed the corridor and made my way onto the stage and gasped as I looked out into the auditorium. All the beautiful painted boxes in white and gold had been ripped out and replaced by, what I presume was to satisfy the designer's less-easily classified libido, a wall of black leather boxes styled similarly to the Barbican and a sea of black leather seats. At the back of the auditorium were two vertical strips of blood-red silk providing the same splash of colour as the red dress of the little Jewish girl in the otherwise black and white film *Schindler's List*. I stood motionless, gazing on this act of progressive vandalism for some time, before making my way to what had been the most gloriously rich, ornate foyer where we drank champagne after the concert with Serge Baudot.

What destruction hath he wrought upon the gilded white pillars, the ornate painted ceiling and the huge gold and crystal chandeliers that illumined the diamond earrings and champagne glasses of the ladies? What Dalek City monstrosity lay in wait? I hummed the Psalm 46 that I had just borrowed from and practically burst into it when I reached the Foyer.

"The Lord of Hosts is with us, the God of Jacob is our refuge!"

"M'sieur?"

A waiter was polishing glasses in the beautiful gleaming Foyer, completely restored to its former glory, with all the slightly down-at-heel decadence it once had, now looking like new. "They kept it!" I shouted and my voice reverberated off the gleaming marble floor. He smiled and looked up at the painting overhead.

"Oui Monsieur, eets wonderfool."

Lyon Opera House

Don Giovanni was not too taxing for the chorus but there was a concert booked that had been dreamed up by the assistant chorus master, another English musician, called Alan Woodbridge. The concert was scheduled for December 17th. It was a programme of Christmas a capella choral music, mostly Twentieth century. This was out of the comfort zone of many opera singers both stylistically and in the difficulty of the actual music. Lassus was OK. John Taverner, two hymns to the Virgin, just about OK. Francis Poulenc's *Un Soir de Neige* and *Quatre motets pour la fête de Noël* were pretty difficult but at least they were in French and some of the singers had done them before. *A Boy was Born* by Benjamin Britten is in medieval English and contains six movements of some of the hardest and unrewarding choral music I have ever encountered. In rehearsals, the French singers were practically crying! We rehearsed in the Église Notre Dame de Saint-Vincent where the priest apologised for the unusually cold weather (about -15 °C) and the fact that the church's heating had been unequal to the challenge but they were trying to get it fixed for the concert! We turned up to the concert; it was snowing outside so it had warmed up a bit, wrapped in overcoats, scarves and gloves. Notwithstanding the extreme cold, the good and hardy citizens of Lyon came in numbers, so we had to proceed, even though the heating engineer had failed to revive the ancient system. We were 26 in the choir and we soldiered through the programme as gradually, more and more of the audience slipped away with a gentle genuflection until the audience and choir were about equal in number. The music was hard enough even in a warm studio but here we were shaking and trying to turn pages with gloves on. We still had the Britten to sing when finally, a French soprano blurted out, both in English and French, that we simply couldn't continue without suffering from hypothermia. Some people in the audience stood up and started clapping and the muted thud of gloved hands brought Woodbridge to his senses and he announced that we would cut the last work, the Britten cantata that ran for about 20 minutes. No man ever made a more popular decision and to this day, I have never performed the work nor heard it performed anywhere since.

For the final performance of Don Giovanni, I took Alex backstage for the closing chorus of the wicked Don being dragged down to hell, which we sang offstage. She watched, mesmerised, her first opera and just a week before her first birthday! It was nearly Christmas and time to go home.

Chapter 24
A 'Proper' Job

We arrived back in Earlsfield, SW18 on December 22nd and were in for an unpleasant surprise. Inside the front door was a pile of post and most of it was from NatWest Bank. The charming Mr Pinney had been made redundant just before reaching his retirement age after a lifetime of service devoted to the bank. A new young manager had been appointed and he wanted to see me urgently. The time I had spent in Lyon had been expensive, what with a mortgage at home and a high rent in France, and the salary from the opera meant that I had just about broken even. I raced up to Wimbledon to see the new manager, who turned out to be almost as charming as Claude Pinney but with a steely no-nonsense side to him. I came out of the meeting realising that I needed to generate some income and quickly. The bank would cover us over Christmas but that was it. I bought a stack of newspapers and began scouring the jobs adverts for anything I could do. *The Stage and Television Today* was a luvvy actors paper favoured by 'resting' thespians looking for auditions. Out jumped a job that had my name on it. It was for an entertainment manager at the Grosvenor House Hotel in Park Lane. I didn't have time to apply in writing, so I phoned up and, as they had heard of me in the business, I was offered an interview right after Christmas.

I think it necessary at this point to say a few words about Grosvenor Productions, in order for the reader to understand how this extraordinary franchise operated. In 1994, the Italian Lord Forte had just handed over control of his vast hotel and catering empire to his son Rocco. Some of the hotels they owned included, The Cafe Royal, Browns, The Hyde Park Hotel, The Waldorf and the flagship, Grosvenor House in Park Lane. It also owned a string of hotels across the country. Within the offices of The Café Royal, there operated a franchise called Grosvenor Theatrical Productions Ltd., a booking agency for events and productions. This was overseen by a tall, suave character, with the

Italian name of Mike Gelardi, who had married into the Italian Forte family and was being 'looked after' by Lord Forte. The real hands-on work, however, was done by his number two, who looked like a bouncer, was a martial arts expert, and spoke without moving his mouth. His name was Jim. His genius was buying in a show for incoming American travel groups, putting it on for next to nothing and selling it to the Americans for literally tens of thousands. Apart from the band of the Irish Guards, the standard of the entertainment was generally not top drawer, but the Grosvenor House was his stomping ground. Despite having this monopoly, the turnover in the year before I joined the company was declared at just £125k. I couldn't imagine how this could be possible. At my interview, the Director, Mike, said that I was what was needed to open an office in Grosvenor House and keep an eye open there to find out why so many corporate events were going to 'outside' production companies. I could tell that Jim was not happy about this and he gave me a pretty hard time at the interview. What sold it was that the Banqueting Director at Grosvenor was an extremely volatile and unpredictable character but whose snobbish nature would be approving of my public-school manner and accent. His name was a word meaning 'shy' (a misnomer if ever there was one!) but I shall call him Mr 'C'. I started at once in January, when it was quiet, so it afforded me time to get my feet under the table. It wasn't long before I found out where the work was going. One evening, working late in a screened open-plan office, a tail-coated banqueting manager came up from the Great Room into what he perceived was an empty office. He was, actually, only about three feet away from me, and I heard clearly as he phoned a company in the King's Road, giving its director every detail of a new big event that had just come in and discussing the payment that would be made directly to his bank account and the balance if they won the tender. He added that Grosvenor Productions had no idea yet about this event. *So!* I thought, brown envelopes all round. He left to return to the dinner event downstairs leaving me to photocopy the file before replacing it in his unlocked drawer. I taxied home and sat up late sorting out a proposal. I won the contract.

My year at Grosvenor House passed quickly and apart from one or two notable trips abroad, I practically lived there and became a well-known figure on the London entertainment scene. I jealously guarded every event that came through the doors by buddying it up with the sales team, so that I knew about a client long before it went into a file, which made me quite unpopular with several banqueting managers, whose brown-envelope-income had been effectively stifled.

One such absence was to go to Venice with the band for a wedding. It was not just any wedding; it was the wedding of my friend Fiorenza to a handsome vet from Umbria. We took a strong team, including my tenor chum Andy Busher

and an organist, as we were performing the church music as well. The wedding was to take place in St George's Anglican Church which was just off the Grand Canal. The bride was to walk in to Vivaldi's Concerto for two Trumpets, played by my chaps from the band, Mike Lovatt and Paul Jayasinha with Bruce Ogston, from the Ambrosian's, on organ. Bushy and I sang the duet from 'The Pearl Fishers' which was an odd choice as it was in French and was about two men who loved the same woman swearing lifelong friendship and saying that no woman would ever come between them!

After the service, we all boarded a flotilla of gondolas with the musicians in the lead boat. The Armada of some forty gondolas set off up the Grand Canal, with me trying to get the gondolier to sing but was saddened to hear that he came from Bulgaria so didn't know any Italian songs. I took over the job and just loved the acoustics with my voice belting out *O Sole Mio*, echoing off the ancient brickwork on either side. Every bridge was packed with tourists, with cameras snapping at this fabulous regatta of smartly dressed people; the family had requested we all arrive in evening dress so we could go straight from the church to the reception without the need to change. After a lovely ten minutes, we reached the Pallazo Pisani Moretta where Mike and Paul had the inspired idea of playing *Rule Britannia* for two trumpets as we came in to moor. The American tourists on the bridges clapped and cheered with delight. The Venetian baroque interior was stunning and the marbled floors brought a welcome cool after the fierce late afternoon sun, reflecting a dazzling light off the waters of the Grand Canal. The air was heavy with the scent of a thousand blooms as the florists had not stinted nor sold themselves short of their best work. I expected a glass of champagne on the trays but what was offered instead was a drink spawned from Harry's Bar in Venice in the late 1930s. This drink is a purée of white peaches mixed with ice-cold prosecco, invented by the owner, Giuseppe Cipriani. He named the drink after a fifteenth-century painting, by Giovanni Bellini, of a saint whose toga had this distinctive pink colour. I took a sip of this delicious cocktail and the only words to describe it would be 'buoni da morire' in Italian which means 'this is to *Die* for!', which it was. In keeping with the Venetian Carnival spirit, it didn't matter if you downed this delicious drink too quickly as there was a fountain nearby that gushed more Bellini!

Unfortunately, I had to sing later. The rest of the band had also arrived by this time and Steve, the drummer, came up to me with a worried look to tell me that Tony, our cultural attaché from Essex, had cornered Sir David (Father of the Bride) to regale him about his story that his real father was, in fact, an Italian gondolier! Sir David was fascinated by this and so I didn't attempt to pull Tony away. Some 15 years later, after much ribbing from the band, it transpired that Tony was re-united with his Italian brother, whom he had never met, and his real father, who lived in Venice, and was by profession, yes, a card-carrying Gondoliere!

After a sumptuous dinner of which I can only remember that truffle made an appearance, we descended back down to the reception area for the dancing. Before we started, Andy Busher sang (beautifully) a love song by Giordano called *Caro mio ben* and there were moist eyes. The band and I then had the rest of the night to play dance music for the guests. At about half-past midnight, we played *A Nightingale Sang* as, like the Queen Mother, it was one of Fiorenza's favourite songs and then we closed. The band was keen to go out and play however and I heard that Sir David joined them for what was quite a rowdy time in some late-night bar. I didn't go as my wife was expecting our second child and it had been a long day with much standing. The following day a huge ferry had been hired by Sir David to take all the guests out to an island to continue the celebrations. A number of people said how much they had enjoyed the music and, as the band were all on board why couldn't we play for them some more.

The answer came back, "Yesterday they were working, today, they are my guests." This was a man who had played the cornet in nightclubs with Sandy Shaw and appreciated musicians. We reached the island and decanted from the huge ferry. There was a lovely club-like place where a sumptuous buffet was served. My Italian friend from Vogue Milan, Carlo Ducci, said it was a shame we did not have 'Volare' in the repertoire and I fully concurred and promised to learn it. The boys had brought their instruments 'just in case' and at the end of lunch, it was announced that the bride and groom would be leaving by a small launch and the brass section, now with Mike Innes on trombone, played a lovely trio version of Rod Stewart's song *Sailing*, as they chugged off in the afternoon sunshine to cheering guests.

Chapter 25
Grosvenor House and Litigation

I returned to my post in Park Lane and things began to hot up regarding the workload. I was asked to look after the very elegant Hyde Park Hotel and also, the privately-owned Park Lane Hotel with its fabulous art deco lobby and ballroom. It was fortunate that all three hotels were within half a mile of each other; Park Lane, Piccadilly and Knightsbridge, so I was able to keep an eye on events even if they happened simultaneously. There were too many of these to recount here but some of them stick out in the memory. One was an event in which I saw why Jim was regarded as a bit of a genius when it came to novel productions. Although it was technically now my hotel for entertainment, Jim had insisted that all corporate travel incentive events in Grosvenor House would be handled by him. That was fine by me, especially as, on a hot July weekend, it left me free to fly to Germany, with the band, for a one-off gig. I returned by Sunday lunchtime to a message asking if I could lend a hand, which I was more than happy to do. We started in the middle of Park Lane, on a sweltering afternoon, by having the guests, about 30 of them make their way onto the grassy central reservation where they were served champagne and serenaded by a gypsy jazz trio and very often, an obligato toot of a horn from passing taxis in the quite busy W1 traffic. I managed the guests through this health and safety nightmare as Jim was nowhere to be seen and we had to stop all the downward traffic from Marble Arch, in three lanes, to get the guests back across the road and into the hotel foyer. I couldn't understand why he had booked 'The Great Room' for 30 guests. As we walked into the long foyer of 'The Great Room' the sight that greeted us was the gleaming blue Williams FW16 Formula One car with the significant number 'O' on the nose. It could only be owned by the aspiring world champion, Damon Hill, team leader for Rothmans Williams and victorious in the recent Monte Carlo Grand Prix, after the death of his colleague Ayrton Senna in

May at the San Marino Grand Prix. Sure enough, at that moment, Jim appeared from the Great Room accompanied by the tall lean figure of Damon Hill, son of the legendary Graham Hill. We ushered the guests into the Great Room which had been halved in size by a huge curtain. The dining table was raised up ten feet off the ground and the room was filled up to that depth with dry ice under-lit with moving blue lights. At a distance was another podium on which there was a white grand piano and a rather nervous Bruce, who had been with us in Venice, who I had booked to sing and play from the American Songbook. He looked uncomfortable and didn't like the fact that he was some 15 feet above ground level, which amused Jim very much. After a really inspired dinner, in which there were no corners cut, I wondered how Jim was going to close. He thanked the guest of honour and asked the guests if they would like to be able to tell their children that they had actually driven against Damon Hill. Whilst talking, the dry ice was sucked out by the air-conditioning and flashing lights were visible behind the curtain, which was raised to reveal a complete Fairground Dodgem system with about 15 cars. *Well done Jim!* I thought, *inspired*. I left with the vision of this world-class driver cramped into a bumper car with a pretty girl squeezed in beside him. Hilarious!

The Autumn was incredibly busy leading up to Christmas and I found myself having to deal with a great many events at the same time. One of the largest, and one which I had to pitch against other established production companies, was for a major City bank called Morgan Grenfell plc., who wanted a Christmas party for 1,600 people! This one was going to take some careful handling. The brief I had was that they wanted a Christmassy theme but one that didn't involve religion as the company had a very diverse workforce, from many different cultures and religions. I got my lightbulb moment from the side of a London bus going past the Houses of Parliament. It displayed a long poster advertising the big family Christmas film coming soon as *The Lion, the Witch and the Wardrobe* after the book by C.S. Lewis. In case you don't know the book, it involves a family of four sibling evacuees from 1940 who are sent to a large house and start by playing hide and seek. The youngest hides in amongst the coats in a deep wardrobe but then discovers it is a secret opening to a parallel world of snow, fauns, dwarves, a wise Lion and the essential wicked witch. I read it to my young English class in '76 when I was teaching and they loved it. It was a tricky one to sell but the Morgen Grenfell committee loved the idea and it being so topical, agreed it would be a great 'icebreaker' to have all the guests decant from their taxis in Park Lane, descend the stairs to the foyer and be checked by security before allowing them to enter a huge wardrobe filled with giant fur overcoats.

The Great Room at Grosvenor House – basic layup for 1,000 diners

By late October, I was told I had won the contract but the Banqueting Director expressed misgivings on my theme idea. I also had to deal with a difficult American agency in regard to another large banking event in February for Cazenove & Co. The CEO of Cazenove had put his secretary and Head of Administration, Mrs Diana Pinn, in charge of the arrangements and I met her with the Banqueting Director, Mr 'C'. She was a very impressive lady who I immediately warmed to and enjoyed the fact that Mr 'C' positively tied himself in knots every time she spoke to him. By the end of the meeting, I had a very clear picture of what was needed for the entertainment. She had wanted 'The Four Tops' but had been over-ruled by her boss who had said he thought Dionne Warwick would be the one to get. I agreed with her; Dionne Warwick's repertoire was mostly written by Burt Bacharach including *Walk on by, I'll say a little prayer, Do you know the way to Saint José?* All very nice, easy-listening songs but as the main entertainment to a slightly inebriated room of 1,200 bankers? Maybe not. My advice was disregarded. If the boss wants Dionne Warwick, then he must have Dionne Warwick. I said I would check availability and come back to her with a price 'delivered'. That meant the whole package including flights, transfers, and included Burt Bacharach and his band but not production, which meant that all sound and lighting would be done by us. That night I sent a fax out to William Morris inc., Hollywood's most powerful entertainment agency who represented both Dionne Warwick and Burt Bacharach. They were also famously, the most litigious firm in the global entertainment business. A representative of WMA must have been working through the night as the following morning, there was a very positive reply to my fax saying that both artists were available and that a delivered price would be £85,000. On top of this, I had to mark up a margin for Grosvenor Productions. Mrs Pinn agreed without hesitation and said that the CEO would be pleased so I assumed that it was all a done deal. I faxed back confirmation, subject to contract.

At 4:00 am, on the morning of December 22, I stepped out of my taxi into a foggy and cold Park Lane and was delighted to see there was already a flurry of activity around the entrance to The Great Room. Some 30 to 40 Christmas trees, 16-foot pines, were being delivered into the foyer, where a huge groundsheet had already been laid, and carpenters were already starting to assemble the vast wooden wardrobe that had arrived flat-packed. By 7:00 am, there was a small forest covered in snow and a lamp post (as per the book) filling the walkway of the Great Room foyer, with its only entrance via a large coat-filled wardrobe. Meanwhile, inside the Great Room, all the rails were being swagged with green and red silk and the sea of ten-foot round tables were being covered with red and green tablecloths, ready for the beautiful seasonal table centres and candelabra. By midday, the sound crews started to arrive for both the Great Room and the Ballroom. By 2:00 pm, the various bands began the long afternoon's sound checks which had to be made in both rooms. It was essential that we had a carousel of live music so, when one band finished another came on and that band would rest until the band in the Ballroom finished a set and the rested band from the Great Room would then take over from the Ballroom. That way the guests in the smaller room didn't feel they were getting a lesser deal. I had booked a number of bands which included the great soul voice of ex-Drifters, Bill Fredericks with my Swing band (jobs for the boys) and a great trio of black lady singers from Birmingham known as 'The Divas'. This was the 90s and Soul music was very big. I had also booked Capital Radio's star DJ, Dr Fox, in the Ballroom from midnight until 2:00 am. The guests arrived at 7:30 and as soon as the shrieks of "Oh wow!!" were audible I knew my eccentric theme was a successful ice-breaker. Once they had passed through the forest and snow machine, they entered The Great Room, which looked stunning with the rear, winding staircase, occupied by 16 boy trebles, and the altos, tenors and basses from the Guards Chapel, where I sang on Sundays. The sound of Christmas Carols wafted up to the Great Room bar where iced champagne was being served. "What's this?" I hear you say. A fortnight before the event, the Morgan Grenfell committee had gone back on their 'no religion' brief and had decided that what it really needed was a choir singing Christmas Carols – but as secular as possible! All dressed in red cassocks and white surplices, they looked and sounded beautiful and set the atmosphere for a great party. Bill Fredericks, backed by my great brass and saxes, wowed them with his '*My Girl* and *Bad Leroy Brown*' and the Divas had everyone up and dancing to *We are family*. At midnight, a rammed Ballroom was ready to greet the guest DJ and I took great pleasure in announcing over the microphone: "Ladies and Gentlemen, the Doctor is in!" At a quarter to two in the morning, I was about to leave when Richard Elliston, the Group Company Secretary, grabbed my arm and shook my hand heartily. "Great party, Graham, great party!" I climbed the stairs to the banqueting office to find a poe-faced Banqueting Director who asked me how I thought it had gone. I replied that I was delighted and so was my client, to which he rounded on me with a straight rebuttal of "this is not up to Grosvenor House standards". I had been up for 24 hours, I had sent 1,600 people away happy, it was 2:00am on December 23rd and I might just make it to bed by 03:00 to grab a short kip to be able to be up to share my daughter's second birthday with my wife, who was nine months pregnant. I got up, turned on my heel and as he was about to continue, left him with a closing:

"Good night and Merry Christmas!"

I returned to work after Boxing Day to find some post on my desk including a large heavy FedEx parcel. I opened the letters first, which included one dated December 23rd, from the company secretary of Morgan Grenfell, who positively gushed enthusiastic thanks and praise as to how well the evening had gone. Considering he was still in the hotel at 1:45am on the morning of the 23rd, I found it amazing he had taken the trouble to write such a lovely letter that same day. I made a photocopy which I placed on the desk of the underwhelmed Banqueting Director who had not yet returned to work. I was feeling smug as I began unwrapping the parcel, which turned out to be what I expected, a very long and detailed contract from William Morris inc. in Hollywood. There wasn't much else pending so I began to plough through this sea of American legal jargon, making notes as I did so. When it got to the payment section there was mention of 'the attached Rider'. I hadn't noticed any attached rider until now but there, sure enough, was an A5 piece of super lightweight typing paper with a hand-typed, rather faint appendix to this contract, attached by a single staple so that it faced outward. Expecting this to perhaps outline any dietary requirements of the artists I was soon put right as to the nature of this rider. It was nothing short of an outrageous attempt to pull a fast one. Agog, I read the transport details listed that included four return first-class flights Los Angeles/London, six business class and sundry economy flights, which they would fix, at an additional cost of £45,000 to us. I read and re-read to make sure I was quite sure that this meant what I thought it meant. I checked my correspondence on my computer and sure enough, there it was in unambiguous black and white, a done deal at £85,000 'Delivered'. Unfortunately, there was no one to discuss this with. The directors of Grosvenor Productions were on leave, as was the Banqueting Director, and I had no intention of appraising Mrs Pinn of this news until I had taken a second or third opinion from a colleague. A few days later, the Banqueting Director returned to work and I ran it by him. Curiously, he was very quiet and I was very surprised when he said we will call a meeting with Mrs Pinn but I think she might be quite pleased. We met on the Friday afternoon and I ran the news by her, watching her face carefully. She displayed no emotion. The Banqueting Director, however, decided to put in his best thespian performance in order to impress her. The general theme was of total outrage and "how dare these Americans think they can behave like this and don't they know who they are dealing with, this is Grosvenor House and the client is Cazenove" etc.

Then he crossed the line:

"Write and tell them that the deal is off, we do not wish to proceed and we are appalled at the way they have treated us. Then make inquiries as to the viability of bringing over 'The Four Tops', who Mrs Pinn had wanted all along!"

He was quite red in the face and I glanced at Mrs Pinn, who knew what I was thinking. This was not his call to make. I suggested that before we get into a legal tangle with the most powerful entertainment agency in the world, we might check to see that it hadn't been a clerical mistake by a minion who didn't understand the word 'Delivered'. But his ego was in overdrive and he raised his voice to say:

"No! It is too late for that, they know what they are doing and, if they don't then, we don't want to be dealing with them. Please arrange for the management of 'The Four Tops' to provide a quote and tell Ms Warwick and Mr Bacharach that we no longer require their services." At that, he suggested they both went off to look at some suggested menus and I was left alone. I got up and left the hotel and went home to think. This was one of those matters that required careful thought and I couldn't say, "What's to be done, Jeeves?" as I was on my own. I didn't want to stress out my wife, as she was expecting to give birth at any day, so I brewed it in my head and decided that, before I started to book any other international artists, I had to go back to WMA and see if I could resolve this. I sent a letter out saying that both my client and I were extremely surprised and unimpressed that the contract sent to us appeared to have added half as much again as was originally agreed and that said client was being strongly advised by a third party (Mr 'C'), to pull out of the deal. I received a strongly worded reply, clearly written by a lawyer, stating that the travel fares were never part of the original agreement and, that any deviation from the contract, as stated, would constitute a breach of that agreement in which WMA would take matters to court to recover the whole amount. I replied in a simply worded letter that we would not be proceeding with the booking and as their contract stated, that it was legally binding unless written objection was received within 14 days, they could kindly take my letter by fax (on the 12th day) as such written objection. I thought that it was no coincidence that this spurious contract had been sent out over the Christmas and New Year holiday season to wind down the clock. Sure enough, a furious legal letter arrived by post from a firm of lawyers representing WMA saying that, as Burt Bacharach had loaded a tour to Italy and Austria on the back of this flight to Europe, he was now suing Dionne Warwick as, presumably, his musicians were suing him for cancellation fees. They added that they were taking this case to the US Federal Court in Los Angeles on behalf of William Morris inc. as Warwick (Plaintiff) vs. Dalby (Defendant). This was getting a bit thick.

On Wednesday 11th January, 1995, I was at my desk in Grosvenor House, with the rain coming down in sheets. I was reminded of a lyric by Noël Coward *early rain and the pavements glistening, all Park Lane in a shimmering gown, nothing ever could break or harm the charm of London Town.* But it was half-past three in the afternoon and the streetlights were on when my phone rang. It was my wife telling me that her labour had started and she was on her way to St George's Hospital, Tooting with godfather Jeremy de Satgé looking after Alex. I said I would be there within the hour, traffic permitting. The whole office knew my situation and when I shouted:

"Baby's coming! See you tomorrow!" There was a big cheer. The Banqueting Director was not present. I dashed out into the street and jumped into the first available taxi. The driver was a learned old cabbie and when I told him, he replied with a "Right ho, Guv" and made the journey in 45 minutes flat, down some back streets I never knew existed. I was directed to the delivery ward where my wife was lying in a bed, quite alone in the room, with the window wide open. She asked if I could fetch her a coffee. I popped downstairs and shortly after returned to see the expression on her face had changed quite radically. I rushed into the corridor and started shouting. No-one was about. "Incubator!!" I yelled at the top of my voice. "The baby's coming now!" After what seemed an age but was probably only 30 seconds, a deliverance of nurses and mid-wives appeared on the horizon pushing an incubator up the corridor and looking for all the world like a bob-sleigh team. The birth of daughter number two was as simple and quick as the number one had been agonisingly slow and painful. It couldn't have been more than an hour and a half before I was sat in the ward, which was starting to fill up with people, including Jeremy and Alex and her two godparents, Fiorenza and Martin Clarke. I had little baby Cassie in my arms, very quiet and peaceful. We were going to name her after my grandmother who had just died but whose first name was Bertha, so we swerved that one and decided that her second name of Cassandra would be perfect. On the table next to where I was holding Cassie, lay a large black brick-like object with a rubber spike protruding from the top. In the mid-nineties, this monstrosity passed for a mobile telephone. This object suddenly lit up and startled the new-born with a vulgar ring. Quickly passing the tiny bundle, that was Cassie, back, I picked up the phone and answered in a whisper:

"Hello?"

The rasping voice of an incandescent Banqueting Manager screamed down the line, "Mr DAAlby!! Where the **** are you? I've been with Mrs Pinn at 6:00 this evening, where the ****were you?"

I explained that I was in the delivery suite at St George's Hospital and that I was whispering because my one and a half-hour old daughter was sleeping soundly. "I don't give a ****!! When you get into work tomorrow morning, you can clear your desk!" [Slam of phone noise].

Most of the people in the ward could actually hear this screaming and language and asked who on earth the lunatic was. I told them it was the

Banqueting Director of The Grosvenor House, Park Lane and I think I had just lost my job.

I made the journey into London the following day by car and duly removed my personal things from my desk. The ladies from the sales department came and expressed their disbelief adding: "But he knew where you were, we all told him the circumstances."

At this time, I had worked exactly 11 months and two weeks and the HR department for Trusthouse Forte were quick to point out that, as I was not yet on a full contract, I had no case for unfair dismissal. But, if I was no longer the Entertainment Director for Grosvenor House, then the pending court case in Los Angeles would have to be Warwick vs Banqueting Director! At home, I was surprised to field a call from Mrs Pinn who expressed her deep regret that I had clearly been used as the fall guy but said that, obviously, there was nothing she could do about it. It was agreed that I would take two months paid severance as long as I was able to help the Forte lawyers to get WMA to drop the case. I took a job offer with a theming company in Battersea that I had booked a lot recently. Every other day for a fortnight, the Forte lawyers would call me at work and record our conversations regarding my paperwork with WMA. After a while, they told me that my paperwork and documentation had been thorough and as the American lawyers could not pick holes in it, they had decided to drop the case altogether, realising they would lose. Mike Gelardi, the director of Grosvenor Productions, took me out to lunch at the Brassèrie Napoleon in The Café Royal. We sat down to lunch after a glass or two of champagne, just the two of us, as Jim was not there and we left at around 8:30 that evening. There had been no expense spared as Mike clearly felt that I had not been well treated. I poured out of the taxi in Earlsfield with the relief that it was finally over.

Chapter 26
New Directions and
Ballroom Dancing!

My work with 'Greenpalms', the props company, was comparatively straightforward compared with Grosvenor House, and I still looked after the independently-owned, Park Lane Hotel. There were some wonderful events including the launch party by Disney of the first video issue of Snow White. It was a lavish event and my band played a whole selection of Disney songs from the 1940s, in original archive arrangements. They loved us, of course! Also at the same Park Lane ballroom, I was asked to play music for a post premier viewing of the beautiful Attenborough film *Chaplin* where we played his own compositions *Smile* and *Limelight*. Michael Caine was very impressed and said to me he never knew Chaplin was also a talented composer.

"Not a lot of people know that!"

During the early Spring, I was contacted by a sound engineer from EMI Abbey Road Studios who informed me of a Portuguese producer who wanted to meet me to discuss a business proposition. I drove up to St John's Wood that evening and found a parking place outside a large house which sported a blue plaque and, even though the house was set back, I could read it: "Sir Thomas Beecham, C.H. 1879–1961, conductor and impresario lived here". I paused with an intake of breath. There was no single conductor in the history of music for whom I had greater respect. His impact on British music was huge and between 1910 and 1950, he was the most important musical force in Britain, founding the Royal Philharmonic and London Philharmonic Orchestras and introducing so many unknown composers, such as Richard Strauss and Frederick Delius to the British public. This was where he entertained composers that included Sibelius and Grieg and on his 80th birthday, having received telegrams from the Queen, the presidents of France, Italy, USA and the Pope, he then asked wistfully, "nothing from Mozart?" I snapped out of my reverie and thought *well, this may be a good omen*, and wandered over to the famous zebra-crossing that led to Abbey Road studios. Alec, the sound engineer was waiting, tall, thin and scruffy with eyes and skin the colour of one who had been working 22-hour shifts, for some considerable time, without sunlight. We went downstairs into a meeting room and I was introduced to a small man of Hispanic looks whose card announced him as being José Calvario, from a Portuguese record company. It was all a bit confusing but, it seemed, a Dutch CD production company, not a label, had decided it would be a good time to get in on the great European craze for ballroom dancing, that was just starting and had commissioned Calvario to fix musicians to record a series of albums on the cheap to cover practically every genre of ballroom dance. We were looking at about 14 albums to be recorded in a week as Abbey Road was very expensive to hire.

I had two weeks to find all the music arrangements, do the costings, fix the players, work out what additional instruments we needed for differing styles, and work out a fierce recording schedule. The Slow Foxtrot, the Foxtrot, Quickstep and the Jive could practically all come out of our repertoire, which we all knew so well and could record quickly. The Tango was trickier and required violin and accordion as well and there was very little music available. The Latin dances such as the Samba, Cha, Cha, Cha, Rhumba and Bossa Nova were all doable but required extra percussion such as congas etc. The Waltz stretched me somewhat as our line-up was all brass and saxes but with a single violin. But the one that had me in absolute despair was the Pasodoble. Pasodoble is a Spanish dance which most people would associate with Bullfighting music, played by town bands from Madrid to Mexico. Before the wonderful world of Internet, this music would be impossible to find. But throughout my life, it seems, God or my guardian angel or whoever comes up with a miracle, when all hope seems lost, came up with the goods yet again. I had met a charming chap at Alex's nursery school and he kindly invited me around for a drink, where I met his lovely Spanish wife, who worked for the Spanish Embassy in London. I asked her about Pasodoble and she became quite animated, saying it was a very passionate Spanish dance that you never hear played properly on 'Come Dancing' programmes in England. She said she would make enquiries from Madrid for me. A week later, a huge box arrived from some official source in Madrid with no name or contact number. Inside were 20 of the most fantastic arrangements for town band of real authentic Spanish Bullfight music! By the skin of my teeth,

I had all the music and the musicians ready to start this epic recording session of seven days. We set up in Studio 2 and quickly learnt the one thing I hadn't been told; we were recording on two-track for speed, so there would be no mixing afterwards, to keep costs at a minimum. I reminded the boys that it was just how bands used to record in the 30s but they reminded me that, if one musician made one mistake anywhere during the track, they would have to stop and do the whole thing over again. This mountain just got a lot higher. The first few albums took longer than I had hoped as the engineer needed time to get the balance absolutely perfect, given that he couldn't edit anything once it was done. The boys had some difficulty with José's name, which was mispronounced José Calamari, instead of Calvario, so they settled on referring to him as Joe Squid! When we came to the Pasodoble album, we brought in a castanets specialist and the results were astonishing. All the albums are now available to hear on Spotify (Graham Dalby and the Grahamophones) and are all of a high standard but the one of which I was most proud was the Pasodoble. You hear it and you think you are in Spain. I gave a CD to my Spanish lady-friend from the Embassy and she too was astonished. It was a tour de force but the huge anthology of dance albums was completed on time and both I and the band were amply rewarded. I stole away with the girls for a fortnight in the sun! The albums I counted on Spotify numbered 18, including the compilations.

In the Summer, I had a deluge of band bookings for one single weekend, seven, in fact. It was the VE Day weekend of 1995 so the 50th anniversary and ten years after our first gig for Francis Mander at the Hammersmith Palais in 1985. Everyone was screaming for props and bands who could play authentic songs of the war other than just Glenn Miller. I hired myself an officer's uniform from Angels and Berman in Shaftsbury Avenue. I knew all the British songs from the time including all the big sing-alongs such as *Hang out the Washing*, *Run rabbit Run*, *Wish me Luck* etc. We set up under the Arches, close by HMS Belfast. Everyone was in uniform; the weather was fabulous and we played four separate concerts. Only on Sunday were we asked to do something just a little different. It was an American incentive group who had asked for the theme of 'Last Days of the British Raj'. We had a stage with great palm trees, a huge 3D tiger-head, crossed polo sticks and pictures of Raj polo teams. My orchestra was set up in the centre. For the reception, I had hired two marvellous Indian brothers called Patel and kitted them out (again from Angels and Berman) in magnificent blue uniforms with white turbans and gloves of the famous Bombay Lancers.

Standing there with their ten-foot lances and pennants, they made an imposing spectacle and the Americans rushed to them to have their pictures taken before even accepting the champagne on offer. My client came over to me and said, "Oh Graham, they're marvellous! Where on earth did you get them from?"

"My dear, we've had them flown in from Mumbai at enormous expense!"

I had paid them each £100 for 45 minutes to stand and be photographed in these magnificent uniforms and, to this day, I believe, Mr Patel and his brother still have their photograph framed proudly behind the counter in their Earlsfield corner-shop. I was in a very good mood that particular day as I was doing well out of this weekend and this particular event was in the Ballroom of Grosvenor House. I was just setting up the band's music stands on the Raj-themed stage when two burly, uniformed, security guards came marching into the room. They called out my name and approached and, although I didn't know theirs, I recognised their faces.

"We got 'im Graham, we got 'im!"

"What? Who? Got who?"

The guard smiled. "Mr 'C'! Everyone was really upset when they heard how you had been treated, what with your new baby and that, but last week, he really put a foot wrong. Apparently, he had been working some sort of wine scam and the General Manager got wise and called him up, whereupon he punched the GM in the face and his secretary called us up to sort 'im out. We frogmarched 'im orf the premises and we weren't too gentle neiver! What goes around comes around, that's wot I say. Nice to see you back."

"Wow," I said, "what happened to the other Graham, the wine manager?"

He had tipped me the wink, there was some dodgy stuff going on when I first started and shared an office with him.

"He was framed and got sacked a month ago."

"Jeepers!"

I now had full closure on the Grosvenor House story.

In the Autumn, I had begun to think of going out on my own and just dealing with music to clients. Several things contributed to this coming to fruition. Firstly, I was called in to, what had been, the Hyde Park Hotel to meet the new General Manager of what was shortly to become the first Mandarin Oriental in London. I arrived wearing a double-breasted pin-stripe suit from Turnbull and Asser, my Old Dovorian tie and a pair of gleaming half brogues from Church's in Jermyn Street. A lot of building work was in progress as the hotel was being converted from a Forte Hotel into a Mandarin one. I was ushered into the office of the new GM, seated behind a brand-new desk with some of his banqueting staff.

"Ah! Come on in, Mr Dalby, so you're the music man?" said a soft, genial Irish accent from behind the main desk. He was dressed in a pink Polo shirt, shorts and boat shoes. His staff were all likewise dressed in mufti as the hotel was closed for refurbishment. I burst out laughing and said, "Yes, indeed, but I don't want any of you to feel underdressed!" There was general mirth and the ice was broken. I recognised two members of staff who had evidently applied to stay on under the new management, an Italian and an Austrian called Werner Anzinger, and he it was, apparently, who had sung my praises to the new GM. It was quickly explained to me that they would like to use my expertise as their supplier for entertainment, once the hotel was up and running and this included seven nights a week of light jazz in the bar plus all the weddings and functions.

The second piece of good fortune was that I had met a tall, lean Londoner called Mel, softly spoken, a workaholic and a stickler for quality and detail. He had impressed some very important clients and was already starting to build quite a portfolio. His company had pitched for the Morgan Grenfell contract and was impressed that I had won it on the strength of my own ideas and music suggestions. At a corporate drinks event, he got chatting to me and said that they needed someone to help them out on a freelance basis, with the entertainment for their corporate events. The company was called 'The Finishing Touch' and was growing rapidly. These two contacts by themselves would provide me with enough work to go it alone. At this stage, I decided to set up a limited company and register for VAT. The amount of work that started to pour in was very considerable and I had to keep coming up with novel ideas for these top-drawer clients. I formed a fantastic function band designed for the larger corporate events. It was fronted by a powerful blond singer from Barnsley called Marie Wilson, who is now well-established in America and a second-generation West Indian singer called Jenny with an amazing soul voice to rival anything by Roberta Flack or the others of that generation. The guitarist in the Grahamophones, Dave Holmes, turned out to be a very talented male lead vocal and an outstanding *Clapton-esque* guitarist. I added my rhythm section of piano, bass and drums and a trumpet, a trombone and a tenor sax all from the Swing band. We did our first gig at the Hippodrome in Leicester Square and was thrilled that my confidence in them was not misplaced. They were fantastic and went down a storm. The name I gave them was perhaps a little strange but it got them talked about. 'METHUSELAH!' always with the exclamation mark. People had to ask why they were called that and I would reply "because there are eight in the band". When the puzzled look did not fade I would say, "Think champagne; two bottles is a magnum, four bottles is a Jeroboam but eight bottles is a Methuselah, eight fizzing artists in one band!" I invested some money in a demo CD and pulled a favour from the sound engineer at Abbey Road, who had done very well out of the ballroom anthology. We spent a whole day in the studio and recorded all the favourite hits of the day. During my time at Grosvenor, every decent band in England had sent me their demo but none of them had anything to touch this. The other thing I did was to contact an old gent in Manchester who ran a business called 'Stars in Your Eyes Agency', after the TV talent show of the same name, and had all the winning lookalike artists who had won the competition on his books. I would put together a 90-minute, after dinner show, using four of these artists with a live band. A typical line-up would be Cher, Meatloaf, Freddie Mercury and Rod Stewart. They would be in full costume and make-up, and they really did look and sound very like the originals. Mel was ecstatic that we had something novel and high quality that nobody had yet seen. His clients, such as Accenture and Deutsches Bank, employed very hard-edged women to organise their events. During this time, Mel was their golden boy, with me delivering the goods, which was not the ubiquitous ABBA cover bands, of which there were about 50 on the circuit! I took this group to some huge venues around Europe including Monte Carlo and Vienna. At Vienna airport, they looked nothing at all without the full make-up and costume, all except the Rod Stewart. He was from Leeds, slightly built with his hair just like Rod's and was a genuine ringer for the original. We walked from the baggage claim to the airport terminal. There, a sizeable gathering of boys had formed a throng around a figure, sporting a red baseball cap with a Ferrari logo above the peak, and was signing autographs. It couldn't be anyone but Michael Schumacher, Austria's Formula One Ace. We walked past, dragging our wheeled cases, and I noticed one lad nudge his friend and call out "Rod Stewart!!"

In a moment, we were being pursued by the whole group of lads clutching their autograph books and leaving the unfortunate racing driver astonished and alone.

I was always on the lookout for new bands with something different to offer and, on one occasion, a party planner asked me to find a band that was really going to knock the socks off a crowd of young, hip, media-types who had seen it all before and were hugely blasé about cover bands. I had been given the nod by Pete, one of my saxophonists, who had stood in for a band who rejoiced in the name of 'The Funking Bar Stewards'. He said, not only were they fantastic but he was paid three times as much as I paid so they must be charging serious money. I said that I did five-star events and didn't think they would be quite what was required at Claridge's or The Dorchester. I kept the demo he gave me without listening to it. This particular event was at the very trendy Café de Paris in Leicester Square, so I gave the tape a spin. It was very good indeed and their cover of Bohemian Rhapsody was astonishing. Could they do it live though? I took the advice of the well-known agency 'Bookem & Riskit' and signed them up for a decent fee.

The Café de Paris was no longer the venue that had hosted Noël Coward and Marlene Dietrich, nor dance bands that included the ill-fated West Indian band leader Ken 'Snake Hips' Johnson, who was killed there at the height of the Blitz. The last time I had been there was in 1988 to take part in a film, *A Handful of Dust* by Evelyn Waugh with Derek Granger producing and Charles Sturridge directing with my band playing *Sooner be a Crooner* to a dance floor of extras dressed in lovely 1930s' costumes. Kristin Scott-Thomas was seated above on the balcony playing bored society wife Brenda, in a full-blown affair with the ghastly and penniless Mr Beaver, played by Rupert Graves. Then the building was somewhat down at heel and still much as it had been during the war. Now, however, it was all lasers and UV lights and smart lights for the disco floor. So sad. My Funking Bar Stewards took to the stage dressed, mostly in black, to some blasé, lukewarm applause which rapidly changed to cries of admiration as they pumped out *Bohemian Rhapsody* live. The energy of the performance built and built and, as they came to the finale, I made my way to the back and the narrow corridor that led to their dressing room. The cases of cold beers I had organised were all there in a large ice bucket. They all came charging down the corridor to howls of appreciation and fell upon the cold beers, whilst ripping off their sweat-soaked clothes, and spraying the cans of cold beer over each other. As I was dressed in a smart suit, I thought it an appropriate time to leave this mêlée of young, sweaty testosterone. Closing the door behind me, I was immediately aware of a presence in the crowded corridor. A tall, dark, good-looking cove, with immaculate stage stubble and expensive cologne, was looking to catch my attention.

"Are you their manager?" he asked.

"Well, yes, for tonight, I suppose I must be as I booked them for this event. Do I know you?" I asked, sure that I recognised him but couldn't put a name to the face.

"George Michael," he replied, "would you mind if I popped my head around the door to tell them it was a great set?"

"George Michael! Yes, of course, sorry it's dark down here. I'll just check to see they are decent." I opened the door and narrowly avoided being hit by a not-quite-empty beer can. I had to shout over the euphoria of post-gig high and singing.

"Guys! Guys!! Guys!!!!" The chorus of *We love you Graham, we do,* died down and I was able to say, "Guys, I've got George Michael outside who would like to thank you for your performance." Uproar and pandemonium with more beer flying in my direction amid the hilarity of my joke. I opened the door and you have never heard eight musicians go silent quite so immediately. A tanned, stubbled, smiling face, with dazzling white Hollywood teeth, left the lads standing gobsmacked in their white underpants, and the only sound was a beer can dropping to the floor. "Great set guys, you did a really first-class gig, cheers."

The door closed to whispered expletives and wide-eyed amazement as they looked at me with newfound awe.

"Wow! Graham, how did you pull that one off?"

"Not a problem, it's what I do, I market bands. I'll deduct the dry-cleaning for the suit from your gig-fee if that's OK?" [Silent nodding]

Chapter 27
Good for the Goose

Chartley Castle, Staffordshire

1996 was a strange year insofar as I spent much of it working on just two projects. The first was a commission from the wife of the new Sheriff of Staffordshire, Mrs David Johnson, to write and compile a huge Son et Lumière, involving the entire history of Chartley Castle, from earliest times. This involved so much research before full production, then the recordings of period music, sound effects and then stuntmen in costume to act out the history. John Touhey, as always, narrated the script which included a scene where Mary Queen of Scots, incarcerated there, was discovered in the famous Babington Plot, to be absolutely complicit in a conspiracy to commit regicide against Elizabeth I and to have England invaded by Catholic Spain. She was then executed at Fotheringhay. As the history came through the Civil War, the Boer War and the two World Wars, I thought we would include fireworks and a thunderous recording of Land of Hope and Glory, from a vast sound system to the three hundred guests in the marquee, watching the show taking place in the ruins of the castle, on a blustery July evening. I then planned for a lone piper up in the perilous, crumbling tower to pipe a Lament for Mary Queen of Scots. Then it went off script…

Mrs Johnson had invited her brother to the event but he was very unwell and when she went to visit him in hospital, he had said how sad he was not to be able to attend but that he would be there in spirit adding, enigmatically, "in some shape or form". In planning fireworks in a public place, you have to seek Council approval and we were told that all fireworks must be done by midnight, so the great finale was timed to start exactly five minutes before. As the music and the smoke died away, it would have been exactly midnight and away across the ha-ha of the castle and up in the highest remaining turret, we had positioned Major 'Dixie' Ingram, Pipe Major, Scots Guards. He started playing his Lament at around one minute past twelve which lasted about three minutes. Just as the skirling, haunting sound was about to finish, an apparition of white came out of the black night sky from behind the piper and flew low over him, so he could feel the beating of its wings. It headed towards the lights of the marquee and directly at the spectators, who ducked instinctively, causing some of the ladies to shriek and laugh. At the last moment, the great, white Canada goose pulled up and soared just over the marquee, and away up into the night sky, to the gasps of the guests. Dixie came down off his turret and called out to me.

"What was that?" he shouted.

He didn't miss a note despite nearly having his Glengarry removed. I explained about the kamikaze Canada goose with the massive wingspan and we had a good laugh over a whiskey, traditionally served to a piper after he's played. I stayed the night at a B&B close by and after breakfast, Mrs Johnson phoned to thank me for the amazing night. She noted the goose and said that she had been called by the hospital last night to say that her brother had died just after midnight and the time of death was pronounced at 12:02 am…"In some shape or form!"

If you enjoy history and are interested in reading my slightly tongue in cheek *Story of Chartley*, it is available online by typing in Chartley Castle and going to the link 'www.aboutbritain.com/towns/chartley-castle.asp' where the Staffordshire Tourist board 'borrowed' my script without asking but I then made them put my name at the bottom. What a cheek!

The second project was to record a belter of an album using some of the great arrangements of the Swing Era, scored and transcribed especially for us. The label was to be EMI and the studio? Where else but Studio 2 at Abbey Road. I had owned a wonderful Land Rover Discovery, which had been stolen just outside Harrods in Knightsbridge and with the insurance claim, I bought a temporary banger and invested the rest into the cost of the arrangements and the session fees for the boys. The album was released in 1997, just in time for our spectacular visit to China and Hong Kong to see it for the last time as a British colony. It was released under the title *Great Legends of Jazz and Swing* and then re-released with extra tracks and better artwork entitled *Swing Classics*. The album contained almost entirely American material and was designed to go with a concert programme I was preparing. This charted the history of Jazz and Swing from Scott Joplin through Paul Whiteman, Duke Ellington, Bunny Berrigan, Benny Goodman, Glenn Miller, Artie Shaw, Tommy Dorsey, Frank Sinatra, Bobby Darrin, Bing Crosby and Louis Armstrong. It was, and is, a fabulous album of which I am incredibly proud. EMI records were woefully poor in promoting it and seemed to only have time for their very troubled star artist, Robbie Williams. The individual playing was just the best standard the band had ever been and we were now ready for an historic trip back to the Far East to watch the Union Jack come down, finally, over British Hong Kong.

Chapter 28
Where the Sun Never Sets

The Wall Street Journal headlined: *"While Britain and China haggle over the hand-over ceremony, hundreds of Hong Kong socialites are booking their ballrooms. Ted Marr, a Hong Kong-based lawyer, has been planning his series of 'China Coast Balls' since October."*

I had alerted the boys that this was not one to miss and had assembled my A-team after receiving Ted's invitation to fly out to play at this historic event. We all had to traipse along to the Chinese Embassy in Portman Square to get our visa applications processed and watch with interest as the news revolved around one story only, The Handover! Ted had organised a trio of events starting with a palace in Beijing. We flew China Air and had an amazing flight over Moscow of just 12 hours from London to Beijing, where the partying had already begun. The guests had been on a walking trek along the Great Wall of China and were now mostly in their rooms cooling down, getting showered and preparing to don their best glad rags for this evening's ball. Ted was in the hotel foyer, cigarette dangling lazily from one hand, with the other clutching a generous sized Gin & Tonic. At the sight of Susanne and me, his face lit up with excitement, and he leapt to his feet to greet us. To order a brace of G&Ts for us was, with Ted, the work of a moment, and the waiter was hastened off, nodding frantically, in the direction of the bar. His wide smile changed to a look of concern suddenly as he gave us the sad tidings that he had been given that morning. Apparently, Ted had unwittingly upset some official or other regarding the music and he had been told that the permit to have a foreign band performing in Beijing had been revoked, although he was allowed to use a local orchestra consisting entirely of violins. It seemed, suddenly, that having Jazz and Swing so close to the Forbidden Palace, had upset the sensibilities of some stuffed shirt CCP official. This was shocking news after a long flight and Ted could sense my disappointment. As ever, he had a plan B to cheer us all up. My wife and I would be invited to the Ball, which had now become a dinner and the boys in the band would be given a cash per-diem to go out on the town and enjoy themselves. I broke the news to the boys, who were delighted that, instead of having to work after a 12-hour flight, they were going to have a sponsored night on the tiles. Not a hard one to sell!

The Forbidden City, Beijing

Susanne and I now had some time before we were to appear, dressed in our finest. I wanted to see the amazing Forbidden City, the home of the 'Last Emperor', Pu Yi. We left our hotel and walked over to Tiananmen Square, the site of the famous anti-Government uprising in 1989 with the famous 'student facing down a tank' image. On arriving, however, I was distraught to discover that the Forbidden City was closed to visitors after 5:00pm, which it had just turned. It reminded me of the trip I once made out to Versailles to discover it was 'Closed on Mondays'! We were flying early tomorrow to Shanghai so there wouldn't be another chance. I couldn't believe it so, when an aged coolie with a rusty bicycle-rickshaw, flip-flops and a straw hat, offered a drive around Tiananmen Square, I agreed. It took about 30 minutes, seated in this squeaking vehicle, and I thought the emaciated cyclist looked as though he had just come out of a re-education camp and was forced to do this ordeal as penance by the Chinese Government, having been caught with an ancient copy of the complete works of Oscar Wilde, left to him by his grandfather. I gazed wistfully at the high stone walls of the Forbidden City and the red-roofed palaces just visible inside. We returned to the hotel on foot, leaving our Olympian dissident clutching some dollars, just a bats-squeak away from a cardiac arrest.

I was soon dressed and ready to go and whilst waiting for my wife, I browsed the tourist brochure advertising the various delights of the hotel. This included a roof terrace bar and as it was a glorious evening, I suggested we went aloft for a quick snorter prior to the dinner. It was a great idea as the terrace was empty, save two white-jacketed waiters who seemed pleased to see us. Then I peered out and over the balcony to what was a full, drone's-eye view, of the sprawling and jaw-dropping Imperial Palace and the out-lying grounds that made up the Forbidden City.

Having seen the best view that Beijing had to offer, we boarded one of those glass elevators and descended to the lobby where a great chattering throng of beautifully dressed party people had gathered, waiting to be bussed to Beijing's Xidan district, which had been classified as a protected heritage site. The venue turned out to be a seventeenth-century palace built by Emperor Kangxi's son. It comprised a stunning, walled courtyard surrounded by four buildings, like many seen throughout ancient China. I didn't know it at the time, but it had been leased by the Hong Kong businessman and socialite, Sir David Tang. I was later to meet the charming Sir David and worked for him on many occasions. I was even invited to play for his wedding party at Annabel's in 2003 and finally, at China Tang in The Dorchester on New Year's Eve 2018, just a year after his untimely death in August 2017. But tonight, he was not present. This was Ted's party.

We were on the last bus to arrive and the party was in full swing with an orchestra of 20 lady violinists in white dresses all standing, playing with no music and all in unison. It looked pretty but really badly needed some harmony. By the lovely gateway into the ancient courtyard, stood an array of immaculate waiters in red jackets bearing trays of vintage, perfectly chilled Bollinger. The night was hot and humid and the champagne slipped down too easily.

We chatted and sipped and sipped and chatted, not noticing that the throng was thinning out, as guests made their way to their tables. Soon, we were practically alone in the courtyard, and we realised we had no idea where we were supposed to be. Each of the buildings was joined by a low corridor, each with a large board showing the seating. None of these included our names. We emerged back into the courtyard somewhat at a loss and asked to speak to one of the head waiters.

"Ah, Mistah Dahbee, you are sitting at Top Table in that biwding," he said, pointing to the only one we hadn't checked. "The captain here wiw show you." A smiling table 'captain' appeared from nowhere and ushered us into the red and yellow lacquered, low-ceilinged chamber. It contained a large, round table, full of guests but with two empty chairs. We slipped quickly into these, hoping not to be noticed and sure enough, the place settings contained little white cards with our names embossed in gold. At such short notice! Just then there was a roar of hilarity from the other side of the round table in Ted's unmistakable Australian accent:

"Aaaah! The Dalby's have arrived! Susanne, this is José, the Cuban Ambassador, and Graham, this is Mercedes, his wife." We shook hands with the respective parties on either side of us. At this moment, my wife's eyes lit up as she had spied a silver Chinese dragon, acting as a table decor, which contained about 50 cigarettes and, on the side, a number of long matches and a striking thingy of sandpaper on its wing. Just then, several waiters, all perfectly synchronised, appeared behind us to fill large, bulbous wine glasses with both red and white wine at our places. This was a 'marvellous party', what could possibly go wrong? Stretching to reach one of the inviting cigarettes, after the first course of delicious Szechuan food had been cleared, my wife succeeded in relieving the silver dragon of one of its cargo and then proceeded, with the other hand, to remove and strike the lucifer on the wing of said dragon. This looked an awkward procedure and sure enough, it involved her left elbow making contact with the un-drunk goblet of red wine in front of the guest seated next to her. The effect of around 30 centilitres of dark claret decanting itself onto the immaculate white silk suit of the Cuban Ambassador was quite a spectacle to behold. I remember it all in a slow-motion moment of abject horror. Quentin Tarantino could have taken her correspondence course: 'how to make a neo-noir film'. The poor man was fabulously cool and unflustered as three, incredibly attentive waiters descended on him, as one of the guests announced with great insight and perception. "Spillage!" and there was polite giggling. Now, there is no way on earth that you could possibly make matters any worse, unless, of course, you happened to be Swedish and therefore, never in the wrong. Whilst I was apologising to the ambassador's wife, who looked utterly horrified, Susanne decided to lay the blame elsewhere:

"I am terribly sorry!" she said. "But it was that stupid dragon thing! Whoever made it has the matches positioned the wrong way, so you have to strike them left-handedly."

The ambassador, without so much as a twitch of insult or injury, replied calmly, "Oh yes, you are quite right. They were a gift from my embassy, but I shall have them taken away and changed, so they strike the other way around. Please don't worry, it is nothing."

Considering she had just trashed a $2,000 silk suit, he took it in a manner which wholly justified his diplomatic status, and I was left in awe of the man, whilst looking for a large hole in the ground.

The China Club, Beijing as restored by Sir David Tang

He later added, equally calmly, that he had another party to go on to afterwards!

The following day we were bussed to Beijing airport, and there we boarded a flight to Shanghai, where we had a few days in the schedule to recover, despite, as yet, having done absolutely no work at all. The band looked decidedly ropey and I gathered, some of them had not been to sleep but had caroused all night. After the episode at the China Club with the Cuban Ambassador, I couldn't get away soon enough, so we had had a reasonably early night. The boys, however, were another matter. We arrived at the Peace Hotel to a splendid reception. Fortunately, we were sharing the coach with a number of the guests of the previous night who were all smartly and elegantly dressed and fortunately, most of them disembarked first, to be greeted by a red carpet, lined with pretty Chinese girls, in too much makeup, all clapping and smiling in a greeting. To one side, was a truly terrible brass band, several press photographers and a TV camera. My dishevelled team followed...our Cornish pianist, Neil Anghiley, excelled himself by falling down the steps of the coach and onto the red carpet and then tripping up Steve Vintner, the drummer coming down the stairs behind him, ending up in an embarrassing mêlée at the feet of the Chinese girls. Once inside the foyer, Pete Whyman, our lead saxophonist, mentioned, casually to me in passing, that he had lost his passport, adding that I shouldn't worry and that it would all be fine. I explained that being a foreigner in Red China without a passport put him on a social standing somewhere between a wharf rat and a man the police had detained in connection with a smash and grab raid (P.G. Wodehouse). I urgently explained this to the horrified concierge who, with great presence of mind, immediately got one of their couriers to go after the coach on a motorbike. Several miles up the road, he caught up with the coach and there, in the back seat pocket, was Pete's passport and visa. Pete remained unruffled as if to say, "There, I told you so".

The Peace Hotel was a magnificent old colonial building but unlike the Peninsula, it was rather rundown and urgently needed modernising. Ted had given Susanne and I a fabulous suite with a jacuzzi and on the rooftop, there was a promenade, nicely lit, to observe Shanghai at night. The great drawback though was that, apart from room service, there was no restaurant, the ballroom being prepared for the great ball the following day. We had to go out to eat. Just a few paces from the busy Bund, you were quickly in a shanty town of great poverty and we despaired of finding a restaurant here, where every street seemed to be a wet market and looked exactly the same. After a while, we reached a Satay House, brightly lit, with Formica tables and garish photos of various dishes that were on offer. Well, I thought, you can't go wrong with satay; it's just chicken on skewers with spicy peanut sauce. I remembered the delicious satay I had been served on the flight to Kuala Lumpur and I was starving. I pointed to the picture and there was much nodding and smiling. No-one spoke Cantonese or English and I had no Mandarin, so it was all about pointing at pictures and saying "Tsing Tao", which was a good Chinese beer. The beer arrived safely and then a huge pile of satay that smelt revolting. Just then, the chef came out of the kitchen, in a coat that had once been white, and sat at a table behind us to read a newspaper. He had a cigarette hanging out of his mouth.

The Peace Hotel on the Bund

The back of his coat was covered from shoulder to shoulder with a yellowish stain of grease and cooking oil and attached to this, were about 300 black flies, to which he appeared oblivious. Susanne looked on with horror. I addressed the plate of satay and offered Susanne to help herself, but she held back. She asked me to try one first and confirm that they were fit for consumption. I picked up a bamboo skewer and bravely took a bite. My face gave everything away. I had never tasted anything like it but there was no doubt, it most certainly was not chicken. Everyone in the restaurant, except the chef was looking at us. I said to Susanne that we needed to eat some of it to save causing offence. At this, she began to laugh then cry! I quickly left a pile of notes on the table and bundled her tearfully out of the door, to the great amusement of the occupants of the 'restaurant'. We walked and walked but no other restaurants appeared until I realised we were hopelessly lost. Finally, I asked some fish vendor and tried every word possible until I remembered that on the Bund I had seen a McDonald's. At this word, his face lit up in recognition and he pointed the way back to the Bund. Incredible that the only word of English understood in China seemed to be a ghastly American fast-food chain, but it saved us that day.

The Ball, the following evening went off extremely well with the guests being very supportive of the band and loving to be able to dance to 1930s' swing in such an Art Deco building. The band finished at 1:00 am officially but kept going with the party until dawn. Finally, we had got to play some music! Now it was time to head off for our ultimate destination and the last few days of British Hong Kong.

We arrived in Hong Kong, eventually, after being buzzed by Chinese Air Force jets, causing the nervous pilot to turn around and head back to Shanghai. He regained his courage, however, and, Dick Whittington-like, turned again and headed on to Hong Kong airport, where we landed without incident. The food in Shanghai had been so poor that the boys all rushed to the airport's McDonald's to grab some fast food. Our hotel was modest after the splendour of The Peace Hotel but given that every hotel on the Colony was fully booked, Ted had pulled off a minor miracle to find us anywhere at all. It was clean and it was central, that was all that mattered. We had a few days to kill before the big night and spent a pleasant time shopping, eating out and enjoying old haunts, such as Ned Kelly's, over the water in Tsim Sha Tsui on Kowloon side.

Our event had been booked for us to get a panoramic view from the Café Deco on the Peak overlooking the whole island. Nobody had predicted the great deluge and the Café Deco ended up shrouded by low clouds, obscuring everything. Fortunately, we had big screens inside so were able to watch the proceedings from a TV viewpoint, like everyone else who wasn't getting soaked. We played during dinner for the guests of Ted's China Coast Ball and then for some dancing as we came close to midnight. I thought *Mad Dogs and Englishmen* appropriate and then, at five to midnight, we played the last number by a British Band in British Hong Kong; it was *We're Tops on Saturday Night* by the 1930s' bandleader, Ambrose, and the title of our very first album. Then we fell silent and watched the screens and the guests, many of whom had lived in Hong Kong all their lives, became tearful. We heard a full-voiced Sergeant-Major give the order to present arms and the slap of 60 hands on rifle butts and the crunch of the left boot being moved behind the right. Then the slow, sad sound of the National Anthem as the Union Jack, soaked and heavy, was slowly lowered as Prince Charles, visibly moved, stood in the salute position until the flag was removed and folded. Patten bit his lip and fought back the tears.

The Central area was full of military and diplomatic types and the world's press were already set up there, around the area for the flag ceremony and handing over after one hundred and fifty years of British rule. The Governor, Chris Patton and HRH Prince Charles were given the unpleasant task of standing, in a deluge of rain, watching the Chinese Party Leaders, ("Appalling old waxworks" as Prince Charles dubbed them!) gloat, as the Union Jack came down for the last time and up went the new flag of Hong Kong. Six hundred Red Army guards presented arms and the flags of Hong Kong and Communist China were raised simultaneously.

At this moment, rather incredibly, the TV cameras swapped to the New Territory border between Hong Kong and the People's Republic of China to view, what looked like, a full-scale military invasion. Hundreds of trucks, containing thousands of troops, were pouring over the border with armoured vehicles. It was an unstoppable swarm of military might. One of the Chinese sound engineers cheered and clapped at this. Steve, our drummer, stretched and accidentally, let slip a drumstick which went whirling silently through the air like the bone in '2001, A Space Odyssey'. The thick side found its mark on the side of the head of the jubilant engineer thus rendering him confused and disorientated for several minutes. That was us done and a glossy American pop band with attractive lady vocalists came on to cheer up the disconsolate guests who, like us, were hell-bent on getting plastered. We had an early flight and by some miracle, we managed to get off the Peak that night and to the airport for the long flight home. Royal Yacht Britannia had sailed out for the very last time. We were to return to perform in 2005 and I am pleased to say that, up to that time, Hong Kong had not yet changed a great deal.

Chapter 29
1998 – Commons and Lords

During my time at Grosvenor House, I had met a number of quite influential people and one such was the Hon. Mrs Caroline Parr, one of the three daughters of Lord Renton. I had done a number of events for Caroline and she was always cheerful and jolly. As this is a book as much about serial name-dropping as my life story, I must include several of her events. The first was a modest event at New Hall in Cambridge to celebrate the 50th anniversary of the girls' college that was Caroline's Alma Mater. There I met the 'fragrant Mrs Archer', as she had just been described by a clearly besotted judge and also her husband, the writer (and soon to be sent down for perjury), Jeffrey Archer. He, of course, was then standing for Mayor of London. He had fibbed to get himself a job teaching at my alma mater, Dover College, who themselves, were too trusting. He had neither been to Oxford University nor held a degree from Yale. But the man can tell a story!

The Great Hall, Lincoln's Inn

The weekend, however, was a success and soon Caroline approached me again, this time to play at Lincoln's Inn for her father's 90th birthday and pretty much, the entire Conservative hierarchy. I was also asked to write a song about the life of her father, David Lockhart-Mure Renton, who served as a politician in the Commons and Lords for 60 years until his death at the age of 98. He was born in 1908 on the 12th of August, which gave me a little starter idea for the song. I set it to the tune of '*D'Ye Ken John Peel*' and, although I've forgotten the words, they started:

"*D'ye ken Lord Renton was born in health in the month of August, the Glorious Twelfth*"!

Baroness Thatcher gave the first speech, which said very little about the birthday boy but rather included a detailed rant against the then Prime Minister, Tony Blair and his foreign policy in the Middle East. The tension was relieved by the second speech, given by Rt. Hon John Major, whose delivery was gently witty and much more about Lord Renton and cricket, which had played an important part in the recreational lives of both John Major and the Host. By the time Major had sat down, after a few well-timed gags, the audience was in a good mood to hear a little comedy. Our trumpeter, Mike 'Magic' Henry, opened with a hunting horn fanfare and off I went with my comic song. I had to pace it quite slowly, as there was an encouraging amount of laughter, and I needed to let them hear the next line. The gags went over surprisingly well and I was greeted with generous applause by the True-Blue elite. I sat down, smiling and relieved, as that constituted what I would deem a 'pressure gig'. Lord Renton then gave a charming speech tinged with sadness that his late wife could not be there with him to open the dancing. He said, "If my wife were here tonight, she would say, '*stop gassing David, and start dancing*' so, come on Margaret!"

With that, he rushed around the table and grabbed Mrs Thatcher, who froze noticeably as she clearly wasn't expecting it. He was a short man but with tremendous energy and with Mrs Thatcher dancing like a tree and him like the comic Judge in *Trial by Jury*, we struck up a good swinging Cole Porter number and off they went to *It's de-lovely*.

I received a lovely letter from Caroline Parr but that was not the end of it. A few days later, my phone rang, it was Lord Renton himself, thanking me for the fine dance music. He added "Apparently, you wrote a funny song about me but

I'm afraid my hearing aid was playing up and with the hub-bub and laughter I couldn't hear a damn thing. Would you be very kind and come and have dinner with me at the House of Lords and perhaps you could sing it again?" I said I would be delighted. And so it was that I spent a delightful evening having dinner in the ancient dining room of the House of Lords. The head of the catering committee at the time was Lord Anthony Colwyn who, apart from being a Peer and a Harley Street dentist, was a band leader like myself and we had worked together at various hunt balls. He was very surprised to see me and greeted me with:

"Glad to see you are moving up in the world Graham, let me know what you think of the catering!" I sang my song and presented Lord Renton with a scroll in a red ribbon onto which I had inscribed the words. After the port and cigars, Lord Renton climbed aboard a brand-new sports car his daughters had bought him for his 90th. He then roared off at speed around Parliament Square and away along the Embankment to his home in Lincoln's Inn Fields. What a character!

The following year, I was playing for the 'Queen Charlotte Ball' charity at the Mandarin when I was asked by two committee ladies if I could donate something for the auction. I pleaded poverty but they said no, I could donate my voice to sing an after-dinner concert with just piano at someone's house. I reluctantly agreed. I was in the reception room with the band with the auction taking place in the ballroom facing Hyde Park. A new banqueting manager, with a striking resemblance to the Fat Controller from Thomas the Tank Engine, came up to the band with the hilarious story that one of the auction prizes was Graham's voice! He expected a good laugh but didn't get it. The boys had worked for me for too long and my band gave them quality work. He suggested he'd start the bidding at 10p. About an hour later, the last course was cleared and the auction commenced. The Fat Controller came in, grinning when the item concerning me came up. He stopped laughing when it got to £100. Finally, he came in again.

"Oh, that's ridiculous! £500! Right gentlemen, start playing, they're coming through to dance." I looked smug.

Several years passed, with no invitation to sing. Finally, the phone rang, it was Caroline. It transpired it was she who had pushed up the bidding and now she claimed my services in the most tragic way. Her younger sister had inherited 'Rett Syndrome' and, severely handicapped, had recently passed away. Caroline wished me to sing at the funeral service. Lord Renton was there, not only as her father, but Chairman of Mencap. Baron Renton of Huntingdon followed his daughter seven months later, just short of his century.

Chapter 30
1999 – The Millennium and Murder Mysteries

I remember 1999 with mixed feelings. Everyone was talking about the coming Millennium and the massive fees we should all be charging to perform on New Year's Eve. But, prior to this, I was to land just a little more good fortune in Life's great fishing trip!

One afternoon, I was loading up the car to go to some gig or other, when there was a shout from my office window from Susanne, telling me that there was a phone call I needed to take. Another two minutes and I would have been on the road. The phone call was, in fact, a secretary from BBC Drama Worldwide, who said that the director and producer of a planned murder mystery series (by the 1920s' author Gladys Mitchell) would like to meet with me to discuss my being involved in an advisory capacity for period music. It is no wonder that I can recall nothing of the gig that night!

I arrived at BBC White City a few days later. I had read up on the writer and discovered she had written 65 novels concerning the lady sleuth, Mrs Bradley. The first, entitled Speedy Death, was published in 1929 and was set in an English country manor house in 1927. By the time I had met the production team, I knew quite a lot about the novels. The researchers, it seems, had found me after looking up musicians who had worked for the BBC on period music, and had found the film *I'd Sooner be a Crooner*, which I had made in 1986. When I suggested that Jack Hylton and his Orchestra had recorded *You're the Cream in my Coffee* in 1927, they jumped at it and asked if my band could record an exact modern replica that they could use as the title music. They also asked if I was free to act as their music advisor for the whole series if the American market took to it. I think this was the best job I ever had!

We spent a productive day recording the title music and other bits and bobs and I was then invited to bring five musicians for a two-day shoot on site. We were to be the band for the engagement party, it seemed, so I brought a pianist, a drummer, a trumpet player, a bassist, a banjo player and me on vocals. I chose the naughty 1927 song by Cole Porter, *Let's Misbehave*. We spent most of the day eating in a double-decker bus waiting to be called. Makeup and costume took forever and by the time they got to us, they wanted to film the band leaving in a huge old Austin with me driving. John Alderton played the host seeing us out and apologising for us not having played. It was half-past ten on a freezing night and I was learning how to drive a car out of a driveway with no clutch. After about five takes and five stalls, I finally got it right and we did a beautiful exit out of the driveway to the shout of "Cut! Thanks everybody, that's a wrap!" Phew! I thought, and so did the freezing crew. We could now go home till tomorrow. When I excitedly waited for this scene, when it was first shown on BBC television, I was devastated to discover it had been cut!

Me with John Alderton   *Colin Goode – Piano, Steve Vintner – Drums,*
Paul Scott – Bass Mike Henry – Trumpet Graham Roberts
– Banjo Graham Dalby – Singer

The following day, we were early into costume and on set where I met the towering figure of Dame Diana Rigg and the benign John Alderton. We did several takes of *Let's Misbehave!* which sounded well. Each time Alderton shouted out "What is that dreadful racket?" In one of the technical breaks, he sidled over to me, rather sheepishly, and said, "Look here, I'm awfully sorry about my shouting. It's er, in the script you see…my line. Actually, I think you're jolly good." Bless him!

Just as it was all going well there was a blood-curdling scream from outside and in rushed one of the servants to say they had found the body of the fiancé dead in the bath. So, this was where we were asked to leave in the large Austin as per the night before. It was all starting to make sense. What I didn't know was that the body, when inspected by Mrs Bradley, turned out to be a woman's body!! How do you get away with that? I very much enjoyed putting together the music for the first pilot and used as much of my own band's material as possible, interspersed with original records from the 1920s from my own considerable collection.

Mrs Bradley Mysteries
'Goodnight Vienna'
Graham – Vocalist
Martin Loveday – Violin
Clive Dunstall – Piano
Paul Scott – Double Bass
Steve Vintner – Drums
Ed Hession – Accordion

The second part of the series was filmed in an all-girls school of which Mrs Bradley was an alumna. I got our pianist, Clive Dunstall, in on it to coach the young ladies who had to learn a scene from *The Mikado*, "Three little maids from school are we". Clive said he quite enjoyed it and when I saw the three actresses involved when it was released, I could quite see why! We also had a very nice scene in a beautiful house in Holland Park, called Peacock House, which was all exotically tiled mosaic and Byzantine arches. It was made out to look like an opium den. David Tennent was playing a suspicious character meeting a woman who turned out to be his mother. We played tangos and included a violin and an accordion for *Jealousy* and *Goodnight Vienna*. Diana Rigg sent the scene up outrageously, after asking her chauffeur where the tango originated, and replying to his shake of the head, "in the brothels of Buenos Aires!" Neil Dudgeon, the chauffeur, then throws a red rose into the air and catches it between his teeth before dancing an incredibly camp tango with Mrs Bradley. When I appeared on BBC's Breakfast TV to promote the series, and mimed to our own soundtrack, they played that section of footage with that quote. When we'd finished, the BBC presenter, instead of asking me about the series, opened up with:

"So, Graham, what can you tell me about the brothels of Buenos Aires?" "Not a lot," I replied and there was a pregnant pause as he fumbled in his notes for another question!

Well, I mean, really!!!

In February 1999, I had accepted an offer of something ridiculously high from Lord Arthur Somerset, CEO of Mask Events, who was directly descended from the Lord Raglan who ordered the Charge of the Light Brigade! Arthur was effervescent and eccentric and I was later to play at his wedding in Raglan.

The Millennium was fast approaching and we managed to move into a much larger house just before Christmas 1999. We had flown out to Finland to see the grandparents and whilst awaiting the return flight at Helsinki airport, my mobile rang to reveal the suave voice of Arthur Somerset. He came straight to the point, which was that his massive event to see in the Millennium, was going to have to be cancelled as all the suppliers, the caterers, the venue and the production people had all been asking for so much money that the ticket prices were through the roof and the punters were just not biting. He then apologised profusely and begged me to accept a 50% cancellation fee. I expressed sympathy for his misfortune and said that that would be fine and quite acceptable. The thing was three months before the Millennium there had been a consensus amongst the musical profession that the going rate on such a momentous occasion to perform would be at least £1,000+ per man. Everyone was holding out for the best offer and highest bidder, which they were sure would be at least that. This meant that I had not yet contracted a single player and so had no cancellation fees to pay out. I boarded the flight back to London in the happy knowledge that I could throw a party for my family in our new house and entertain quite lavishly to include my parents, my sister and her husband and the four of us. In the words of George Formby: "It's turned out nice again!"

The Millennium party in our new house was a great success with literally cases of Bollinger and a five-course dinner and featuring Susanne's truly excellent Beef Wellington. We danced to Scottish reels on the forecourt and could just see the huge firework display coming from the Thames. Our road seemed empty but for an elderly West Indian lady about to walk past. I grabbed the whiskey decanter and offered her a glass with a hearty "Happy New Year!" She recoiled, shocked. "No maan, ah don't drink," she said with a musical, calypso inflexion but I sensed a hesitation. When I pressed her, she agreed to a very small one. I poured a small glass, of this excellent ten-year-old malt, which she downed in one. It was quite dark, but the whites of her eyes widened. After a few seconds, they were joined by a set of pearly whites in a wide grin and a husky Jamaican accent: "Eh, maaan, dat's not bad. I'll take one for de road!" And she allowed me to refill her glass. And with that amusing encounter, we entered the Naughties. It was now 2000. My father was enjoying himself immensely but I wasn't to know that this was the last time I was to see him alive.

The New Year was in fact full of interesting things. My two girls, Alex and Cassie, now went to a posh school in Wimbledon called 'The Study', up on the Common. Alex's friends all had dogs and she had been badgering me for a puppy for quite some time. Finally, I gave in and found a breeder up North who supplied the Andrex Puppies for the television adverts. When the girls saw the pictures, I knew there was no going back; we would have to make the long journey to Mansfield to choose one. During the week, I was enjoying a beer with Andrew Usher and his wife Charlotte. Andrew was Lord Usher from the 'Fall of the House of Usher' fame and was a huge jolly chap who filled a pub. When he heard of the puppy saga and how we needed to think of a name, Charlotte piped up. "I know, why don't you call it Chardonnay?" Everyone roared with laughter and approval except me.

"Chardonnay? My dear Charlotte, you've been watching too much 'Footballers Wives!' This is a full-on Kennel Club pedigree Sandringham Labrador-Retriever and very posh indeed. Chardonnay? More like Bollinger, I should say?" At this, another huge roar of laughter and approval. So, that was decided upon.

And so it came to pass, that our family of four came to be five, with the collection of a puppy so cute that, when I first took her to collect the girls from school, there was a scream from the hundred or so schoolgirls reminiscent of an early Beatles concert. Bollinger or 'Bolly' as she became known, was one of those dogs that just loved life, people and any amount of crisps she could find on a pub floor. She lived a long and very healthy life and finally departed in 2016 being as old as the century and sharing her birthday with me, as mine fell on December 2nd and hers on the 3rd. I would pour a little Bollinger into her bowl and we would share our celebrations

Bollinger 'Bolly' Dalby 1999–2016

Chapter 31
Epilogue – Full Circle

This book opens in 2000 with me and my orchestra at Windsor Castle, playing for the birthday of HM, the Queen Mother, for the second time in my life. Now, another two decades have passed and so much has happened, some of it good and some not. My two best Royal patrons were not long for this world. Princess Margaret left us in February and Queen Elizabeth, the Queen Mother in March 2002.

The BBC had been in touch with me in 2001 to record a programme entitled *The Queen Mum and Me* which was a short 30-minute documentary about various people who had had real-life experiences with this great lady. They got us to record *A Nightingale Sang* in an empty theatre belonging to Fiorenza's brother, Christopher. It was aired at 12:00 midday on 8th April, 2002, during the Lying-in-State. The following year, I was asked by the Middleton family to play for their daughter's 21st birthday where it was clear that this young lady and Prince William were quite besotted with each other. Watching the cenotaph on November 7th, 2020, during the scaled-down service, everyone remarked how one person stood out as a future queen, Catherine, Duchess of Cambridge.

An invitation by The Royal Warrant Holders in 2002 caused me to pick up the classical baton again to put on and conduct a huge concert to celebrate 500 years of Royal music. I was proud that I managed to synchronise the slow march from Pomp and Circumstance March No. 4, in time with the footsteps of Princess Alexandra, as she walked down the stairs into the Great Room of Grosvenor House to be greeted by 1200 Royal Warrant Holders and my one-hundred-piece choir and orchestra.

My youngest daughter, Cassie, following in Father's footsteps, won a scholarship to sing at Salisbury Cathedral for five years. She was signed to

Signum Classics, aged 12, to record a lovely album with the Esterhazy Orchestra. The title of the album is her middle name *Emilia*.

The band changed its name to 'The London Swing Orchestra' for the London Olympics and had some quality trips, to Hong Kong again, Cebu, Jordon, Morocco, Geneva and Rome. Amman, in Jordan, was for Princess Badiya's wedding and Rome was for Valentino's 75th, whose niece, Beatrice Borromeo, wished us to play for her wedding in Monte Carlo to Pierre Casiraghi, son of Princess Caroline. We were asked back by Princess Caroline for the Rose Ball in Monte Carlo and then onto Vienna. We also played in 2019 in Edinburgh for the wedding of Princess Badiya's sister, Princess Basma.

Several years ago, I ran into the same Francis Mander who had caused me to form a band in 1985 and got me to conduct in the Royal Albert Hall. He hadn't changed at all and still spoke with the same boyish enthusiasm:

"This is great, really great, you must come to my Bluebell Party in Gloucester!"

I arrived on a glorious Spring day with the woods overflowing with Bluebells and Francis with a camera around his neck.

"Hey everybody, this is Graham Dalby, he conducted a concert we held in the Albert Hall with a one-hundred-piece orchestra, come and see..."

And with that, he got a crowd of people and ushered us along a corridor where on the wall, was a large, framed photograph of me, looking unfeasibly young, standing outside the Albert Hall and Francis looking well, like Francis. Thirty-five years on, and he hadn't changed a bit!

So, after 40 years of travelling the world as a musician, giving thousands of concerts and meeting all sorts of wonderful people, I have now settled down to conduct amateur and semi-professional choirs around the Wiltshire/Somerset borders, including the Trowbridge Philharmonic Choir and The Choir of the Western Wynde.

My daughters are all grown up now and Alex is a delightful jeweller, operating in Bristol, whilst Cassie is an equally delightful post-grad singer at The Royal Academy of Music. Mutti is still with us, as effervescent as ever at 94. Susanne and I sadly parted company during the dark days of the financial credit crash. After some of what Churchill called 'Wilderness Years', I have settled with a lovely lady called Linda, who loves music and dogs and puts up with me and my foibles. Thank you, Linda x.

****

I should like to thank the nurses and staff, (albeit that most of them have gone on to a greater light) of Great Ormond Street Hospital and in particular, Mr Philip Rainsford Evans (1910–1990), the consultant and paediatrician to H.M. the Queen who successfully saved my life in 1958, thereby making me, I think, the longest living survivor of the catheter procedure, pioneered back then.

I should also like to thank all those musicians who have worked with me in various bands, choirs and orchestras and contributed to the great pleasure we all take in making music and bringing joy and happiness to as many people as possible.

Lockdown project
New CD of the LSO
Release date September 2021

signum
CLASSICS

Emilia

The London Esterházy Orchestra
Conducted by Graham Dalby

Trowbridge Philharmonic Choir
and Orchestra
Conductor - Graham Dalby
Present ~
HAYDN'S
'THE NELSON MASS'

Soprano Siân Dicker, Mezzo Cassandra Dalby, Tenor Ed Coton, Bass Graham Case
Original 1798 version for Strings, Organ, Trumpets and Timpani

After the interval:
Christmas Carols sung in English, Welsh, French and Latin
and Audience Participation as is now traditional !

St James' Church, Trowbridge
Saturday, December 14th 2019
7:00pm doors 7:30 Concert

Tickets: £12.50 (includes programme)
online: www.ticketsource/......
Tel: 01225 766573, from choir members or on the door

The Boys in Dubai in some publicity poses for the Great Ormond Street Appeal on a very hot day!

2020/2021 has been a very hard two years for all musicians and for us both, and I conclude with the fact that Linda and I were both locked down, having tested positive for COVID-19 but, vaccinated now, we will beat it, and in the words of Richard Strauß:

"Und Morgan wird die Sonne wieder scheinen." (And tomorrow, the Sun will shine again).

Mozart Anniversary Concert, 5th December 2021, Wiltshire Music Centre

Graham Dalby's book opens inside Windsor Castle at the 'Ball of the Century' in 2000 in which he drops so many names it's hard to keep up. He then takes us through his precariously dangerous childhood from Nigeria, Singapore, and Hong Kong where he served for a short while as a police inspector. The rest of the book is Dalby's fast-paced life of classical music and jazz and swing and is a case-book study on how to manage to drink champagne belonging to the rich and famous.

His style owes much to P.G. Wodehouse and Evelyn Waugh but the historical interpolations keep the reader in the realms of reality and fact. An incredible story of great anecdotes and a page-turning read with laughter and some tears but mostly music, champagne and laughter.